Easy
LINGO

Easy
LINGO

Jennifer Bennett

A Subsidiary of
Henry Holt and Co., Inc.

First Edition—1996

ISBN 1-55828-487-7

Printed in the United States of America.

10 9 8 7 6 5 4 3 2 1

Trademarks

Throughout this book, trademarked names are used. Rather than put a trademark symbol
after every occurrence of a trademarked name, we used the names in an editorial fashion only,
and to the benefit of the trademark owner, with no intention of infringement of the trademark. Where such designations appear in this book, they have been printed with initial caps.

Associate Publisher: Paul Farrell
Executive Editor: Cary Sullivan
Editor: Andy Neusner
Copy Edit Manager: Shari Chappell
Copy Editor: Suzanne Ingrao
Technical Editor: Mike McGrath
Production Editor: Joe McPartland

Dedication

To all my students—
Past, Present, and Future

ACKNOWLEDGMENTS

I would like to thank the following people for all their help: Robert V. Whitney of Macromedia for giving me a chance; Jono Hardjowirogo for giving me the opportunity to write this book; Andy Neusner for seeing it through; Mike McGrath for making me a better writer; Nilson Neuschotz for no reason whatsoever; Ken D'urso for his dice game; Barbara James for promising to use this book in all her classes; Tommy Oddo for his wonderful Shockwave movie; Nicholas Bennett for his infinite patience and technical knowledge; and Sara C. Sabo who, at present count, has twice given me life.

CONTENTS

Chapter 2:
Pull-Down Menus.............. 25

Chapter 3:
Movies in a Window 45

Chapter 4:
Introduction to Puppets and User-Defined Variables 59

Chapter 5:
Using Puppets to Create a Button Handler 83

Chapter 6: RollOvers 103

Chapter 7: Controlling Digital Video.................. 117

Chapter 8:
Synchronization of Video and Screen Events........... 139

Chapter 9:
Fun with Sprites............. 149

Chapter 10: Using Xtras.................. 165

Chapter 11:
Shockwave Goodies 189

INTRODUCTION

So, you've gone as far as you can go in Director without having to learn the dreaded programming language, Lingo. It's time to make your presentations interactive, but the thought of programming intimidates you. Take heart. Lingo is easier than you think, and this book makes it even easier! This book is put together a bit differently from other Lingo books. Instead of listing a bunch of commands, and asking you to figure out how to use them to accomplish your task, this book looks at the task first and then gives you all the Lingo elements you need to reach your goal. For example, if you want to create a pull-down menu in your presentation, go to Chapter 2 and follow the simple steps and Presto! You have a fully functioning pull-down menu.

This book shows you the step-by-step basics of Lingo as well as more advanced topics. If you are new to Lingo programming, start with Chapter 1. Later, when you feel more confident with Lingo, you can jump to whatever chapter interests you, whether it is creating buttons from your own graphics, synchronizing stage events and video, or controlling a QuickTime movie. If you have a basic knowledge of Lingo, feel free to start anywhere in the book. This book will walk you through real-world examples of Lingo while the CD-ROM contains finished examples and practice files that you can work with as you read. These examples and lessons have been tested in the classroom for ease of use and effectiveness. Using this book is just like having a Lingo teacher by your side.

At the beginning of each chapter, there is some basic information on what will be covered and a list of Lingo included in the chapter. All Lingo is clearly visible so you do not need to hunt through the pages to find the programming code. In addition to the steps to follow and the code to write, there is information to help you understand the basics of programming in Director as well as Director performance tips and tricks.

This book does not try to cover every Lingo element, but it includes the most useful Lingo and gives you a solid base to work with. After you have finished this book, you will be ready to investigate further topics on your own.

It's time to get started. Relax, take a deep breath, and enter the world of Lingo. You will soon see how powerful it is and wonder how you ever did without it.

CHAPTER 1

SIMPLE BUTTONS AND NONLINEAR PRESENTATIONS

Lingo included in this chapter:

```
go to the frame
go to "label name"
go to marker
go next
go previous
play
play done
go loop
```

Linear (li-near) (adj.) 1. of or in lines; 2. involving one dimension only; 3. one heck of a boring type of multimedia presentation.

This chapter introduces you to Lingo and gives you some easy but valuable Lingo commands. We will be constructing a nonlinear presentation using Director's Button tool, frame scripts, and cast scripts. The Lingo scripts found in this chapter are the basic building blocks of Director scripting. They are scripts you will use time and again even after you become a Lingo expert. Enough talk, let's get started!

3

Linear versus Nonlinear Media

So, you're watching a news program, waiting for the one segment that interests you. Unfortunately, television shows are linear. You have to watch the entire television show until you see the part you want. Imagine how nice it would be to see only the parts you wanted and bypass the rest or even watch the sections you like over again. What about a magazine? You see an interesting article on the cover and want to learn more. In a magazine, you can read only the parts you want and skip over parts that don't interest you. Think how tedious it would be to have to read all of the magazine to get to the part you want. Chances are you would lose interest before you even got to the piece you wanted to read and put the magazine down.

Now, think about your linear multimedia product. Your customers have to watch your entire presentation in order to get the information they want. Your salesmen have to demonstrate every aspect of your product in order to get to the information your customers are interested in. Hopefully, when the customers do run across the things they want to know, they haven't fallen asleep or tuned out completely. What you need is a nonlinear presentation. In a nonlinear presentation, the users can look at the elements in your presentation in the order they choose. They can even skip parts completely. A nonlinear presentation manipulates the playback head, sending it to specific locations when asked. To create a nonlinear presentation in Director, you need to use Lingo.

The Lingo you will use in this chapter will give the user the power to watch your presentation in whatever order they choose instead of having to watch your entire presentation frame by frame from the first frame of the movie to the last.

Getting Started

Open the movie **Ch1com.dir** on the CD that accompanies this book. Play the movie. Notice that the movie looks like it is paused. Click the button labeled **Secret #1**. You see an entirely new screen. Click the **Return** button. Now, you're back where you started. Try the **Secret #2** button. Notice that even though it appears as if the movie is paused, the steam from the coffee cup continues to be animated. Click the **Return** button. Try the **Secret #3** button. Again the movie appears to be paused. Click the **Next word** button. One word is now visible. Click the **Next word** button again. Another word is revealed. Each time you click on the **Next word** button, yet another word is uncovered. Click on the **question mark**. You have now branched to a new movie. Click the **Return** button. Now you are back in the **Chap1com.dir** movie. Stop the movie and look at the score, as shown in Figure 1.1.

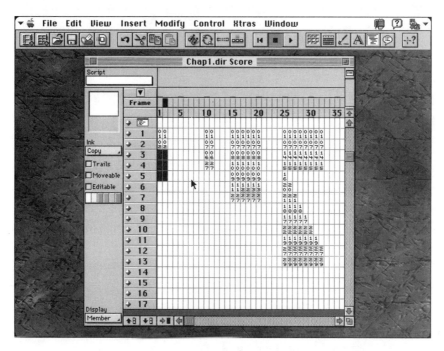

Figure 1.1 The score for the **Chap1com.dir** Director movie.

You will see four sections of animation separated by blank frames. Keep the score open and play the movie. You will notice that the playback head has stopped on frame two. Click the **Secret #3** button. The playback head jumps to the last section of animation without playing the frames in between. The movie uses Lingo to control the playback head. Two types of Lingo scripts are used in this particular movie. One is called a *frame script* and the other is a *member script*. Each one will be introduced in turn as you build the scripts necessary to create a nonlinear presentation.

It's time for you to build in the interactivity in this movie and to start using Lingo.

Open the movie called **Ch1.dir**. The score will look like the one in the movie you were just in. Now play the movie.

You will see all the frames in the movie as they appear in a linear fashion. Obviously, this is not how you want the movie to play. You need to add Lingo scripts to make the movie work nonlinearly. First you will place the buttons in frames 1 and 2. Director has a Button tool to make this process easy.

Creating Buttons Using Director's Button Tool

Stop your movie. In the score, select **frame 1, channel 3**. Choose **Tools** from the Window menu. In the Tools palette (see Figure 1.2) is the button tool.

Select the **Button** tool and click on the bottom left hand part of the stage.

A button appears on the stage with a blinking cursor located in the middle of the button. Type **Secret #1**.

To change the font of the button, first select the text on the button. Choose **Text** from the Modify menu. Select whatever text and text color you want.

With the button still highlighted, you can change the background color of the button so it is not always white. Use the background color chip in the Tools palette to change the background color of the button.

If you are having problems seeing the background color of your button, make sure the ink effect on the button is not background transparent. In this case, a copy ink effect will work nicely.

T I P

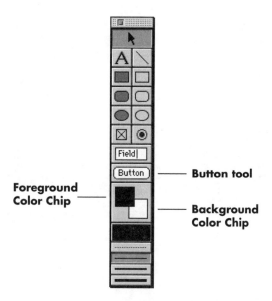

Figure 1.2 The Tools palette.

To copy the cell, click on it to select it, hold down the **Option** button on the Mac, or the **Alt** button on Windows, and drag the cell from frame 1 to frame 2.

SHORTCUT

Copy the button in frame 1, channel 3 into frame 2, channel 3.

Select **frame 1, channel 4**. Create another button in the lower middle section of the stage. This button should say **Secret #2**. Change the button's attributes using the preceding techniques.

Copy the button in frame 1, channel 4 to frame 2, channel 4. Make a third button called **Secret #3** and place it on the bottom right part of the stage, as shown in Figure 1.3.

Figure 1.3 The stage with buttons in place.

Looping the Movie with Lingo

If you play the movie now, there is nothing stopping it in frame 2 so you can click a button. You need to make the playback head "loop," or stay, on frame 2. You will use a frame script to do this. Frame scripts are always located in the script channel of the score.

Select **frame** 2 of the script channel in the score. Click in the **Script Preview** area (Figure 1.4) of the score to open a Script box.

You will see two lines already there. The first one is *on exitFrame*, and the last line is *end*. (see Figure 1.5).

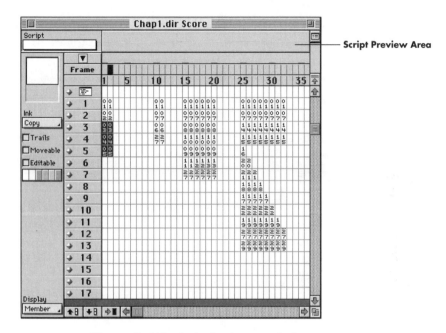

Figure 1.4 The Script Preview area in the score.

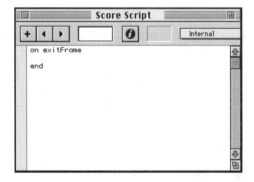

Figure 1.5 The Script window for a frame script.

These lines are the skeleton of a handler. Handlers contain lines of code that are executed upon certain events. In the case of frame scripts, the event can be either *on enterFrame* or *on exitFrame*. The *on exitFrame* event happens when the playback head leaves the current frame it is in. The *on enterFrame* event happens when the playback head is about to enter a frame.

The handler *on enterFrame* will not work if placed in the first frame of a movie. There are too many other events happening that you don't see, causing the frame script to be skipped.

N O T E

A handler always begins with the word *on* and ends with the word *end*. Also notice that when you open a Script window, a blinking cursor is already set between the first and last line of the handler, ready for you to type your Lingo.

Type **go to frame 2.** Your handler will look like this:

```
on exitFrame
      go to frame 2
end
```

Lingo is not case-sensitive, so it doesn't matter if you use uppercase or lowercase or a combination of both.

Close the Script window using the Close box in the upper-left-hand corner. You can also use the **Enter** key on the numeric keypad to close the Script window. (Windows 3.1 users, make sure your **Num Lock** is on.)

It is important for you to always close the Script window before playing your movie. If you have a script error, Director will usually tell you as soon as you close the Script window.

Most script errors are simple typing mistakes. If you have an error, check your spelling carefully, then close the Script window again.

T I P

It's time to see if your script works. Rewind and play your movie. It should stay in frame 2 so now you can click on the buttons.

The script works! You will soon discover that the more general you make your scripts the better off you will be. What if you need to add a few frames to the beginning of this movie to display a company logo? The script still tells the playback head to stay in frame 2, but you may actually want it to stay in frame 4. You would then need to go back and change the script. You can make this code more generic so that it will work in any frame.

Making your Script Generic

Stop your movie. Choose **frame 2, script channel** and open the script by clicking in the **Script Preview** area of the score. Replace the line *go to frame 2* with *go to the frame*.

```
on exitFrame
        go to the frame
end
```

You can think of the phrase *go to the frame* as "look to see what frame you are in and stay there." *The frame* is a function. *Functions* return a value in Lingo. In this case, it returns the frame the playback head is in. To see how this works, choose **Message** from the Window menu (Figure 1.6).

Figure 1.6 Director's Message window.

Inside the Message window, type **put the frame** and hit the **Return** key. The Message window gives back the value -- 2, indicating that the playback head is in frame 2. This script will work in any frame, keeping the playback head in whatever frame it is currently in.

Rewind your movie again and play it. It should work exactly as it did with "go to frame 2" in the script channel.

A Note on Human Interface Guidelines

Notice that when you click a button, it changes colors briefly, then returns to its original colors. Certain objects in every program work according to a set of *human interface guidelines*. These guidelines differ slightly from Mac to Windows, but are generally consistent in software packages. One of the basic human interface guidelines is that a button must change in some way when it is clicked to indicate to the user that the button is selected. Another human interface guideline states that when you select a menu, the menu name "highlights" or changes from black text on a white bar to white text in a black box and the menu items are displayed vertically starting at the menu name. On both platforms, if certain menu items are not available, the item name is grayed out. Most programming that follows human interface guidelines isn't even obvious to you, the user, but it did have to be programmed to act the way it does. When you make a button with Director's Button tool, it will automatically follow these human interface guidelines. When you click on it, the button colors turn into the opposite of the colors shown in the button's "up" or normal state.

So now you have a button but it doesn't really do anything. Next you will place a *cast script* on the buttons to make them branch to different parts of our movie. Stop your movie.

Placing Markers and Labels in the Score

We first are going to place some markers in our score. *Markers* give you a visual cue as to where certain pieces of animation stop or start and are useful when using Lingo. Drag a marker from the marker well to frame 1. Notice that there is a blinking cursor after the marker.

Type **start**.

The name of a marker is called its *label*. You will use the label names in conjunction with Lingo to indicate to the playback head where it should go. Drag another marker from the well to frame 10. Label this marker **#1**. Drag a marker from the well to frame 15. Label this marker **#2**. Drag another marker from the well to frame 25. Label this marker **#3**. Figure 1.7 shows the score with markers and labels in place.

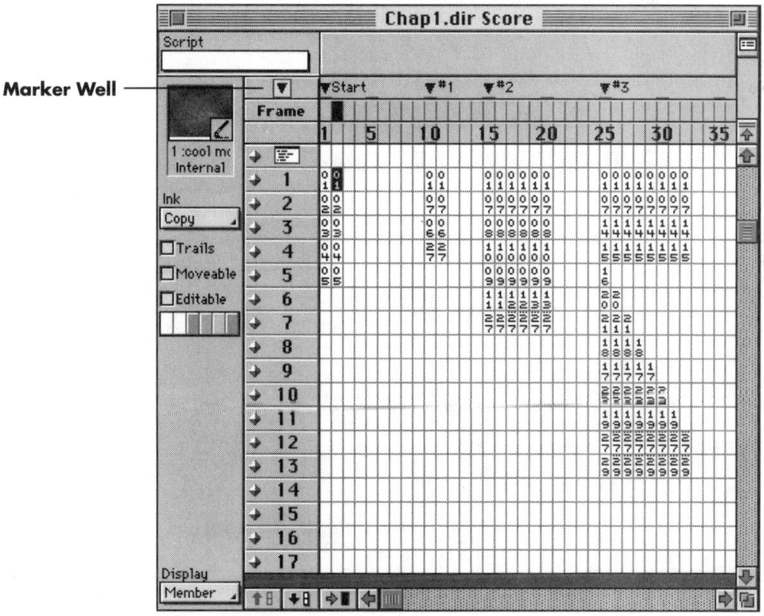

Figure 1.7 The marker well in the score.

To remove a marker from the score, drag it down from the marker row and let go, similar to removing a tab in a word processor.

T I P

Adding Cast Scripts to Create a Nonlinear Presentation

You will now add cast scripts to the buttons to create a nonlinear presentation. Select the button **secret #1** in the Cast window. Click on the **Script** button in the Cast window (Figure 1.8). You will see a different handler. Type **go to "#1"** so your handler looks like this:

```
on mouseUp
      go to "#1"
end
```

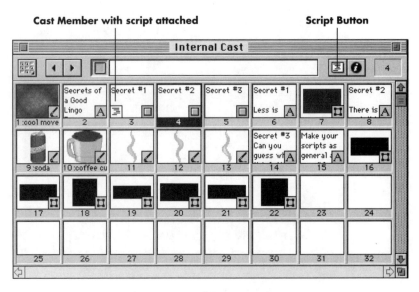

Figure 1.8 The Cast window.

Make sure you put the label name in quotes.

You will only see the handler name "on exitFrame" in a frame script. You are using a cast script here. A cast script usually starts with either "on mouseUp" or "on mouseDown" to indicate when the script will be executed. You will create a "mouseUp" script here. This script is executed when the user clicks the button and then lets go of the mouse button or when the button is returned to its "up" state. A script that executes "on mouseDown" will execute as soon as the user clicks on the button or when the mouse button is held down. You will use a cast script here because we always want the button to do the same thing.

Now you have a frame script and a cast script. How does Director know what script to do when? A cast script will override a frame script so even though we have a frame script telling the playback head to stay in frame 2, when the user clicks on the button, the cast script is activated and the playback head goes wherever the cast script tells it to go.

Notice that when a cast member has a script attached to it, you see a little script icon in the left-hand corner of the cast member in the Cast window.

Rewind your movie and play it. Press the **secret #1** button.

What happens? The playback head does go to marker #1, but then continues through the rest of the movie. You didn't tell it when to stop or when to return to the beginning. You will first tell the movie when to stop so your audience has a chance to read what is on the screen by adding another frame script.

Stop your movie. Select **frame 11** of the script channel and open a Script window. Type **go to the frame**. Then, close the box using the **Enter** key on the numeric keypad. Rewind and play the movie again. Press the **Secret #1** button.

Your movie goes to the section of the score labeled #1 and stays there. Now you need a way to get back to the main screen.

1. Stop the movie.

2. Select the **Button** tool from the Tools palette.

3. Click on the **stage** to create a button. Type the word **Return** on the button. You can change the text attributes and button color if you want.

This **Return** button is always going to return to frame 1, or the "start" label, so we can use a cast script.

Select the **Return** button in the Cast window and click on the **Script** button at the top of the Cast window. Type **go to "start"** so your entire handler looks like:

```
on mouseUp
        go to "start"
end
```

Always make sure you use quotes around a label name when programming, or Director may think the label name is a variable and give you an error message.

Try your movie. Does the **Return** button do what you want it to?

Next, let's script the second button with a cast script.

1. Stop your movie.

2. Select the **Secret #2** button and open a Cast Script window.

3. Type **go to "#2"** so your handler looks like this:

```
on mouseUp
        go to "#2"
end
```

4. Rewind and play your movie. Click on the second button.

The playback head goes to the right place, but again, it just keeps going. It should remain in the #2 section. What happens if you add a frame script that says "go to the frame" in frame 20? Then the playback head will stay in that frame and the animated steam rising from the coffee cup will stop too. You need to create a loop so that frames 15 to 20 keep playing. You could use "go to frame 15." That will work but again, the more generic a script, the better off you will be. Instead of using frame numbers, there is another way you can loop the animation, using markers.

Using Markers and Lingo

There is a numbering system attached to the markers. The first marker to the right of the playback head is marker (1). The marker to the left of the playback head is marker (-1) *unless* the playback head is in a frame that does not have a marker. In that case, the marker immediately to the left of the playback head is marker (0). If the playback head is in a frame that has a marker, that marker is marker (0). This may seem a bit confusing now but it will become easier as you use markers in your scripting.

Working with Markers

If you want to work more with markers, you can try them out in the Message window (**Ctrl-M** on Windows, **command-M** on Macintosh). The Message window is a great place to try out markers. Place the playback head in frame 20 (see Figure 1.9). Type in the Message window **put marker (1)** and hit the **Return** key. The Message window returns a value of 25 indicating that the first marker to the right of the playback head is at frame 25. Now type **put marker (0)** and hit the **Return** key. The Message window returns frame 15. On your own, move the playback head to a frame that has a marker and try different marker numbers, including marker (0), in the Message window and analyze your results.

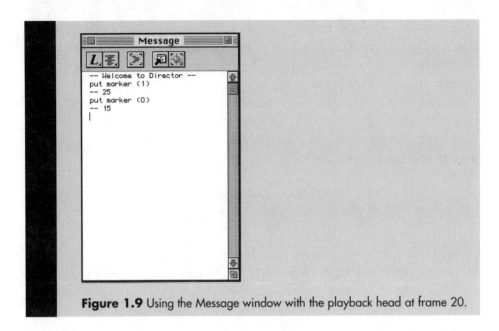

Figure 1.9 Using the Message window with the playback head at frame 20.

There are also some special Lingo commands specific to markers. They are **go next**, **go previous**, and **go loop**. You will use them in this chapter. This last command will return the playback head to the first marker to the left of the playback head. The command **go loop** is equivalent to **go to marker (0)**.

Stop your movie. Open a frame script in frame 20. Type **go loop** so your handler looks like this:

```
on exitFrame
      go loop
end
```

Rewind and play your movie. Click on the **Secret #2** button. Does the animation in frames 15 to 20 keep playing? If not, check your scripts and the placement of your markers. Stop your movie.

You need a way to exit this loop. Adding your **Return** button to the stage will do it.

Find your **Return** button in the cast window and place it on the stage in frame 15. In-between it to frame 20. You want to make sure that the button is available during the entire animation, not just in one frame.

Test your movie. Stop your movie. Select **Secret #3** in the cast window. Add a cast script to it that tells the playback head to go to marker #3. Rewind and play your movie. Press the third button.

Again the playback head goes to the right spot but keeps on going. You need to add a frame script so that the movie doesn't run through all the frames. What you want to happen here is for the playback head to stay on a frame until the user clicks a button, then for it to advance to the next frame and wait until the button is clicked again. So, you need a frame script in frames 25 through 32.

Stop your movie. Select **frames 25 through 32** of the script channel. Go to the Script pop-up menu (Figure 1.10) and select the script that says **on exitFrame go to the frame**.

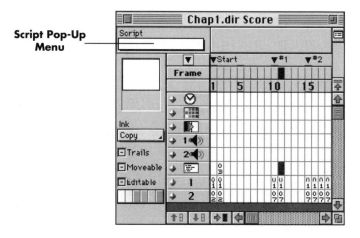

Figure 1.10 The Script pop-up menu in the score.

You might have noticed that after you create a script it becomes a cast member, and you know that re-using a cast member is more efficient than creating duplicate castmembers. When you are scripting larger projects, your movie will look cleaner and easier to follow if you re-use scripts instead of creating them every time you need them.

Your next task is to get the playback head to advance one frame at a time. You'll create another button to do it. Select **frame 25, channel 12**. From the Tools palette, select the **Button** tool and click on the bottom right of the stage. Type **Next word**.

You can change the attributes of the text to anything you want. In-between the button in frames 25 through 32. Because the button is always going to perform the same task, you will attach a cast script to this button. You will use the marker Lingo go next. Select the button in the Cast window and click on the **Script** button. In the mouseUp handler, insert the following line:

```
go next
```

Go next means go to the next marker to the right of the playback head. For this script to work you need to place markers on every frame from frame 25 to frame 32. When the markers are placed on frames 25 to 32, it will look like Figure 1.11.

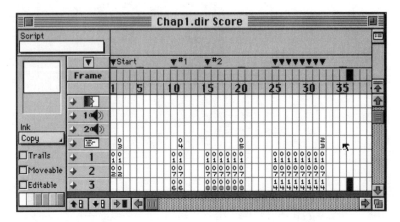

Figure 1.11 The score with all markers in place.

Rewind your movie and try your new buttons.

There is a counterpart to the "go next" script called "go previous." Try adding another push button that uses this script to cover the words one at a time.

Play and Play Done

Next, you will add functionality to the **Help** button. The Help screen is located in a separate movie. This Help screen needs to work a little differently. It is simple enough to script the **Help** button, but what about when you want to return from the Help screen? If you choose the **Help** button when on the Secret #1 screen, you want to go back to that screen. If you choose the **Help** button when on the main screen, you want to go back to the main screen. How will you script a **Return** button from the Help screen to go back to the screen from which you requested help? You will use the **Play** and **Play done** commands. When you use **Play** instead of **Go to**, Director remembers where the **Play** command was issued and returns there when it encounters the **Play done** command.

You will now add a cast script to the **Help** button. Select the **Help** (**Question Mark**) button in the Cast window. Click the **Script** button in the Cast window. Add the following code:

```
play frame "help" of movie "help.dir"
```

Take a moment to look at the score to the **help.dir** movie. The first nine frames are blank. That is why your code tells Director to play a particular frame in the **help.dir** movie (Figure 1.12). If you wanted to start at frame 1 in the movie **help.dir**, then your code would have been:

```
play movie "help.dir"
```

Figure 1.12 The score for your **help.dir** movie.

 Although you are using the **Play** command to branch to a different movie here, you can use the **Play** and **Play done** commands within a movie anywhere you would use **Go to**.

NOTE

1. Save your movie.

2. Open the movie **help.dir**.

3. Select the **Return** button in the Cast window. Click the **Script** button.

4. Type the following command in the *mouseUp* handler:

```
play done
```

5. Close the Script window and save your movie.

6. Open your **chap1.dir** movie. Play your movie and click on the **Help** button. You branch right to the frame labeled "help" in the Help movie.

7. Click the **Return** button. Choose one of the Secret buttons. Click the **Help** button again. Now you are back in the Help movie.

8. Click the **Return** button. You should be back in whatever frame you were in when you clicked the **Help** button.

Play and **Play done** are two very helpful commands for creating bookmarks or glossaries or for any application where the user may need to branch to a certain part of a movie and then return to where he or she began.

You now have a fully functioning nonlinear presentation! Hopefully, now you realize that Lingo isn't so hard. You learned how to loop a movie using a frame script and how to create a nonlinear presentation using cast scripts. Now your customer or end user controls what parts of the movie they see, instead of the other way around.

The scripts you learned here are very common commands. You will see them throughout this book. In the following chapters, you will learn how to add pull-down menus to your presentation, how to play more than one Director movie at a time, how to use external code, and a lot more. You have just scratched the surface of what you can do with Lingo.

CHAPTER 2

PULL-DOWN MENUS

Lingo included in this chapter:

```
installMenu
set the checkMark of menuItem "item" in menu "name"
set the soundLevel
halt
repeat with
```

These days you run across pull-down menus in virtually every application on the Macintosh or on Windows. In fact, you are so used to them that you probably take them for granted. They are used for navigation, editing, setting certain system requirements, and accessing application-specific tools. In Director, they are easy to create and implement. In this chapter you will create two pull-down menus: one for navigation and one for accessing the volume in your system software.

Getting Started

Open the file **Ch2Com.dir** on the CD accompanying this book. Play the movie and try all the menu items to see how they work. The Go To menu navigates you to different frames in the Director movie. Try out the keyboard shortcuts built into the menu. Use the Volume menu to change the level of music; notice that there is a check mark next to the volume level currently in use (see Figure 2.1).

Figure 2.1 The Volume menu.

Open the file **Ch2.dir**. You will find the stage already set and several one-frame animation segments present in the score (see Figure 2.2).

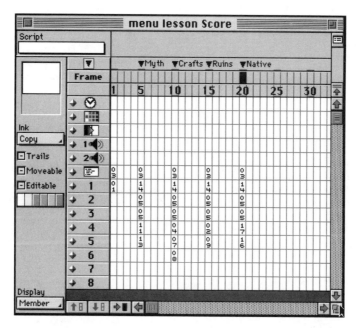

Figure 2.2 The score in the Director movie **Ch2.dir**.

There are also some frame scripts present that you will take advantage of during this chapter. Each frame script is simply the command **Go to the frame**, which was introduced in Chapter 1.

You will start creating a menu. Menus are constructed as field cast members. First, you need to tell Director that you are typing a menu, then you give the menu a name.

Creating a Menu

Choose **Field** from the Window menu. In the Field window, type **menu: Go To**. Whatever is typed after the colon is the name of the menu; it will appear in the menu bar *exactly* as you type it. In general, Lingo is not case-sensitive. However, if you type **go to** in lowercase, that is how it will look in your menu bar. For that reason, you might want to be careful how you type the menu name. The word *Menu* is a keyword in Lingo (see sidebar).

The Elements of Lingo

Lingo comprises a combination of different elements. The categories of elements in Lingo include commands, functions, keywords, properties, operators, and constants; you used some of these elements in Chapter 1. You used a Lingo command when you used **go to** in Chapter 1. *Commands* tell the Director movie to do something while the movie is playing. You used a function when you used *the frame*. Remember, a function returns a value. In the case of *the frame*, the function returned the frame number the playback head was in. In this chapter you will use properties, constants, and keywords. *Properties* are attributes of an object and are always preceded by the word *the* such as *the stageColor*; this Lingo is a property of the stage. A *constant* is just what it sounds like: something that does not change. The constants we will be using in this movie are *TRUE* and *FALSE*. *Keywords* are reserved words that have a special meaning in a particular computer language. *Menu* is a keyword in Lingo; it tells Director that whatever follows that word is a customized pull-down menu. An *operator* is a term that modifies the value of something. In Lingo, there are arithmetic, comparison, logical, and string operators. A simple example is the multiplication operator that takes two or more values and multiplies them together to give a different result.

Adding Lingo to Your Menu

Next, you need to add the commands that you want available under the menu. The actual command name is separated from the Lingo code by a "|" (**Shift-**).

NOTE

The "|" symbol stands for a *logical or* in many programming languages. It's also known as a *pipe* or a *vertical bar*.

Press the **Return** key and type the following:

```
Main Menu|go to frame 1
Mythology|go to "myth"
Native Crafts|go to "crafts"
Ruins|go to "ruins"
Native Peoples|go to "native"
```

Your screen should look like Figure 2.3. The words in quotes are label names that are located in the score. It is important to use the quotation marks so Director will know to look for labels. Otherwise, Director will assume that the words are user-defined variables and will give you an error.

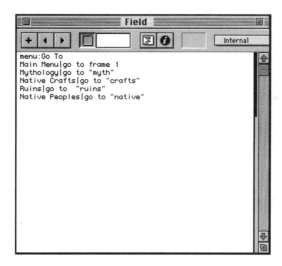

Figure 2.3 Your field cast member with a menu.

Close the field box.

Now you must install the menu in the menu bar using Lingo. Menus are often installed as soon as a movie starts. You could install the menu in a frame script, but there is a better place to do it; you will install the menu using a movie script.

The Movie Script

The movie script is not attached to a particular cast member, sprite, or frame but rather is available throughout the entire movie. Special handlers called *primary event handlers* are found here, as are user-defined handlers. Often, you will find several different handlers within the movie script. These handlers can be called from within other scripts whenever you want them to execute. Because handlers in the movie script can be called from cast, frame, or sprite scripts, handlers that you want to execute more than once are often located in the movie script. In this way, you can write a handler once but use it repeatedly throughout your Director movie. Names of handlers in the movie script need to be unique names that are *not* Lingo elements. You will never see *on mouseUp* or *on exitFrame* in a movie script. You choose particular names for each of your handlers. The names need to start with a letter (as opposed to a number) and cannot have spaces. So if you want to name your handler "Do This Thing," take out the spaces so the name looks like *DoThisThing*.

Director movies can have more than one movie script, although in most cases, it is easier to have only one. That way you don't have to search through several movie scripts to find a handler you need. However, a movie script can only store 32K of information, so if your movie script is approaching this size, you may want to split the information into two movie scripts. If you do need to use more than one movie script, organize your handlers in a way that makes sense. For example, place all handlers that deal with digital video in one movie script and all handlers that deal with sound in another.

Select **Script** from the Window menu and type the following handler (Figure 2.4):

```
On startMovie
     installMenu 14
end
```

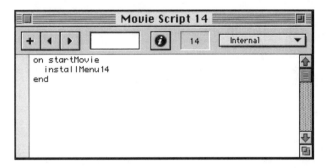

Figure 2.4 The movie script.

Menus are always referred to by their cast number. In this case, your field cast member that contains your menu should be cast member 14.

On startMovie is a primary event handler. When certain events happen in your movie, the first place Lingo looks for instructions to carry out is in a primary event handler. If it doesn't find any instructions there, it will continue looking in other places, such as in a cast member script or frame script. The code within the *on startMovie* handler will be executed as soon as the movie starts—even before the playback head places any elements on the stage— regardless of whether the movie is started at frame 1 or frame 10. Your menu will now be installed as soon as the movie starts.

Save your movie and try out your new menu.

About Keyboard Shortcuts

It's a good idea to add keyboard shortcuts to your menus. Some members of your audience will prefer using them over using the mouse to select a menu item because they can save time.

A *keyboard shortcut* is simply a combination of keystrokes that perform the same task as choosing a menu command. On the Macintosh, the **command** key and a letter key are usually used for shortcuts; on Windows, the **Ctrl** key and a letter key are used.

You will add a keystroke and the letter **M** for a keyboard shortcut. A shortcut created on Windows will work on the Mac and vice versa.

Adding Keyboard Shortcuts

Open **cast member 14** by double-clicking on it in the Cast window. Place the blinking cursor after the word *menu* of Main Menu. Type **/M** (see Figure 2.5).

Figure 2.5 Menu with keyboard shortcut.

You have just created the keyboard shortcut **command-M** for the Mac or **Ctrl-M** on Windows for the menu command **Main Menu**. Lingo equates the slash with the **command** key on the Mac and the **Ctrl** key on the Windows platform.

Play the movie; try out the new shortcut. Save the movie. Now create shortcuts for the rest of your menu items.

Common Keyboard Shortcuts

Many computer applications have adopted the same letters for keyboard shortcuts. On both Windows and Macs, the shortcut key (**Ctrl** on Windows or **command** on Macs) in combination with **X** stands for *cut* with **V** stands for *paste*, with **C** stands for *copy*, and with **P** stands for *print*. Try to stay away from using these letters in your applications for unique tasks; users may think they are copying something when they are actually deleting a file! One product in the late 1980s used **command-Q** to run a script. On Macs, **command-Q** is reserved to quit programs! You can see the confusion that could result here. Use common sense when creating keyboard shortcuts. The shortcuts are supposed to make your application easier to use, not frustrate users.

You're off to a great start! Your next task is to create a second pull-down menu for the same Director movie. All pull-down menus that are visible at the same time are created in the same field cast member.

Open cast member 14. On the line after the **native** command, type:

```
menu:Volume
Mute|mute
Soft|soft
Medium|medium
Loud|loud
```

Your field cast member should look like Figure 2.6.

Figure 2.6 The field cast member with two menus.

We don't need another **installMenu** command because the two menus are in the same cast member, and both will be installed at the same time. The words after the "|" are names of handlers we need to create in the movie script.

The Lingo you use will actually manipulate the sound device that is part of your computer's system software.

Open the movie script. You can either select **Script** from the Window menu or use the keyboard shortcut **command-Shift-U** on the Mac or **Ctrl-Shift-U** on Windows to open the movie script.

Type the following four handlers:

```
on mute
     set the soundLevel to 0
end
on soft
     set the soundLevel to 2
end
```

```
on medium
     set the soundLevel to 4
end
on loud
     set the soundLevel to 6
end
```

The handler names—mute, soft, medium, and loud—are not Lingo terms, they are names of user-defined handlers. They are created by the Lingo programmer. They could have been pizza, cat, and DoIt, but those names would not give you a clue as to what the handlers do. It's always best to give handlers meaningful names so it's easier to find and edit them later.

Notice that *soundLevel* is one word; it is a Lingo term. Many Lingo terms are made up of more than one word. The second word is capitalized only to make it easier to read. Because Lingo is not case-sensitive, it doesn't matter whether it is capitalized. The soundLevel on both Macs and Windows can vary from 0 (sound off) to 7 (maximum volume).

NOTE   soundLevel is a property, or an attribute of your movie. Remember that properties have the word *the* in front of them.

Save your movie, and try out your new menu. Why does the volume change? How does Director know what to do? When you change the volume to loud, for example, Director reads the code after the pipe. In this case, it reads the word *loud*. Because Director doesn't understand the word *loud* as a piece of Lingo, it goes to the Movie script and looks for a handler with that name, executing what it finds in that handler.

Adding Check Marks to Your Menus

In most applications, when a menu item is selected, a check mark appears to the left of the item so that the user can easily tell which item has been chosen. You will add this feature to your Volume menu using Lingo.

Open the movie script. In the "soft" handler, add the following line:

```
set the checkMark of the menuItem "soft" of menu "volume" to TRUE
```

The value of the Lingo property *checkMark* can be either TRUE or FALSE. If it is TRUE, you will see a check mark. If it is FALSE, there is no check mark.

Close the move script, play the movie, and choose **soft** from the Volume menu. Look under the Volume menu again. **Soft** should have a check mark next to it (see Figure 2.7).

Figure 2.7 The Volume menu with a check mark next to **Soft**.

Select **Mute** from the Volume menu and look at the menu again. **Soft** still has the check mark.

Stop your movie. Open the movie script and add the following line to the mute handler:

```
set the checkMark of menuItem "mute" of menu "volume" to TRUE
```

Close the movie script and play your movie again. Choose the **Soft** command and then the **Mute** command. Look at the menu now (Figure 2.8).

Figure 2.8 Volume menu with two check marks.

We have a definite problem: It looks like we have two menu items selected at the same time. We *can't* have the volume on soft and mute at the same time. The check marks are turning on when we ask, but we didn't tell the first check mark to turn off when we selected a new item from the menu. The safest thing to do is to uncheck all items before we place a check mark by the item we want.

Turning Check Marks Off

Open your movie script. Add the following new handler:

```
on uncheck
    repeat with i=1 to 4
        set the checkMark of menuItem i of menu ¬
        "volume" to FALSE
    end repeat
end
```

The line that starts with set the checkMark is one continuous line that ends with FALSE; ¬ is the continuation symbol. Type the **set** command in one line with no breaks.

NOTE

All repeat loops need an **end repeat** command to tell Lingo when to stop executing the commands in the loop. Without the repeat loop, the uncheck handler would look like this:

```
on uncheck
    set the checkMark of menuItem 1 of menu "volume" to FALSE
    set the checkMark of menuItem 2 of menu "volume" to FALSE
    set the checkMark of menuItem 3 of menu "volume" to FALSE
    set the checkMark of menuItem 4 of menu "volume" to FALSE
end
```

It is not too tedious to type these four lines, but imagine if you had ten menu items to set the check mark to FALSE. It's easier and more convenient to use a repeat loop. The line that reads repeat with i=1 to 4 in conjunction with the line set the checkMark of menuItem i of menu "volume" to FALSE will replace *menuItem i* with *menuItem 1*, *menuItem 2*, *menuItem 3*, and *menuItem 4* sequentially. This turns off the check marks on mute, soft, medium, and loud. This type of repeat loop is invaluable when you need to turn several things on or off; it will save you production time and it is easy to edit later.

Uncheck is a user-defined handler name; it is not a Lingo term.

Once you have created a handler, you need to *call* it. You need to place the name of the handler whenever and wherever you want that particular handler to be executed. You will first call the uncheck handler in the handler that is executed to change the volume to soft.

Change your soft handler to look like the following:

```
on soft
    set the soundLevel to 0
    uncheck
    set the checkMark of the menuItem "soft" of menu "volume"¬
    to TRUE
end
```

Now, when someone chooses a new volume level, all the menu items in the Volume menu are unchecked using the uncheck handler. Then only one check mark is applied to the item that has been selected.

Change the other volume-related handlers to work correctly with the check marks. You can write this Lingo by yourself. Just call the uncheck handler in the correct places in the other volume-related handlers. Compare your scripts with the ones at the end of this chapter.

Close your movie script, and rewind and play the movie. The check marks should work correctly. Save the movie.

Setting Initial Volume for Your Movie

Let's set the initial volume level to **Loud** and place a check mark next to **Loud** in the Volume menu.

1. Open your movie handler and add the following lines to the on startMovie handler:

```
set the soundLevel to 6
set the checkMark of menuItem "loud" of menu¬
"volume" to TRUE
```

2. Close the Movie Script window.

3. Save your movie.

4. Play the movie and try the menus.

Let's add one last thing to our menus: a way for users to get out of our presentation. We will add **Quit** to our Go To menu.

Open member 14. Before the line menu : Volume add the following code:

```
(-
Quit|halt
```

The first line indicates a *separator bar* or a disabled line that separates or groups similar terms. Look at your Director File menu. There is a separator bar between **Close** and **Save**. We are using a separator bar here because **Quit** isn't exactly like the other menu items (Figure 2.9).

If you have worked with Lingo before, you have probably seen the Lingo term *Quit*. The **Quit** command will literally quit you out of Director and put you in the Finder or Program Manager, which isn't very handy if you are working on a Director movie. The **Halt** command will simply stop your movie from playing while you are in Director. However, if you have the command **Halt** in a projector, then the projector will quit out to the Finder or Program Manager.

Figure 2.9 Menu with separator bar.

In case things aren't working properly, compare your movie script with the following finished one:

```
on startMovie
     installMenu 14
     set the soundLevel to 6
     set the checkMark of menuItem "loud" of menu "volume" to TRUE
end

on mute
     set the soundLevel to 0
     uncheck
     set the checkMark of menuItem "mute" of menu "volume" to TRUE
end
```

```
on soft
    set the soundLevel to 2
    uncheck
    set the checkMark of menuItem "soft" of menu "volume" to TRUE
end

on medium
    set the soundLevel to 4
    uncheck
    set the checkMark of menuItem "medium" of menu "volume" to TRUE
end

on loud
    set the soundLevel to 6
    uncheck
    set the checkMark of menuItem "loud" of menu "volume" to TRUE
end

on uncheck
    repeat with i=1 to 4
        set the checkMark of menuItem i of menu "volume" to FALSE
    end repeat
end
```

More Menu Options

There are many more tricks you can perform with menus. You can add other customized menus in frame scripts, *disable* or gray out menu items, and format menu items with boldface, underline, or shadow text.

For more information on other menu options, look in your Lingo Dictionary under the heading *menu*, or use Director's on-line help engine. It is greatly improved and a valuable resource.

When you want to remove a menu, use the Lingo `installMenu 0` in a frame script.

N O T E

Congratulations! You have created pull-down menus with Lingo. Next, try adding menus to your own presentations. Customized pull-down menus are a powerful element in a presentation whether you use them for navigation, customized options, or to manipulate system settings like in the volume example here. Remember that you can install menus in frame scripts if you want to add or remove certain menus during your presentation.

CHAPTER 3

MOVIES IN A WINDOW

Lingo included in this chapter:

```
open window
close window
forget window
set the title of window
tell window
printFrom
windowType of window
```

As you have probably discovered, when you are developing in Director, you cannot have two Director movies open at the same time (as convenient as that would be at times). However, there is a way to play more than one movie at a time. It's called playing a *movie in a window* (MIAW). The MIAW plays exactly as it would if it were running alone. It retains all of its formatting, and you can interact with it just as if it were the only movie playing. The original movie that the movie in a window was called from is referred to as the *host movie*.

The uses for an MIAW are endless. MIAWs are ideal for glossaries, customized dialog boxes, and Help files and for showing examples, QuickTime movies, and 3-D renderings of a product. Imagine creating an interactive clothing catalog with a graphic display for every item. When the user finds something he or she likes, he or she can click the graphic and get another window with all the colors or styles of that item as well as a QuickTime movie of a model showing all sides of the garment. What a great marketing tool!

In this chapter, you will learn how to make an MIAW and a printable notepad.

Getting Started

Open the file **MIAW1com.dir** on the CD that accompanies this book. Play the movie and click on the **Glossary** button.

The glossary is actually a Director movie that contains a scrolling text cast member. As soon as you open the MIAW, it is the active window. You can close the MIAW using its Close box in the top-left-hand corner. Figure 3.1 shows the Director movie playing an MIAW.

Look at the pull-down menus. Only the commands under the Notes menu are enabled. Choose **Open Notes** from the Notes menu. Another Director movie opens in a window. Type a message in the Notes window. Choose **Close Notes** from the Notes menu. Choose **Open Notes** again. Your message is still there. Choose **Print Notes**. Your message should print out from your printer (as long as your printer is connected and turned on). Last, choose **Clear Notes** from the Notes menu. Your message is removed. Notice that whenever you stop the movie and start it again, the notepad is empty, ready for the next person to use it. You will learn how to accomplish all these tasks in this chapter.

Opening a Movie in a Window with a Cast Script

Open **Host.dir**. You will add a cast script to the **Glossary** push button to open a movie in a window. In the Cast window, select the **Glossary** button. Then click the **Script** button in the Cast window. Create the following mouseUp handler:

```
On mouseUp
      open window "MIAW.dir"
end
```

MIAW.dir is the name of the movie that contains the glossary. Play your movie and click on the **Glossary** button.

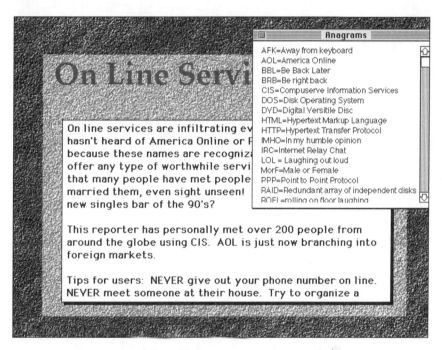

Figure 3.1 A Director movie playing an MIAW.

The movie **MIAW.dir** opens, and the text scroll bars function properly. However, the title bar of the movie says **MIAW.dir** which does not convey any useful information to the user (see Figure 3.2). You can change the title of the window using Lingo while maintaining the actual name of the Director movie.

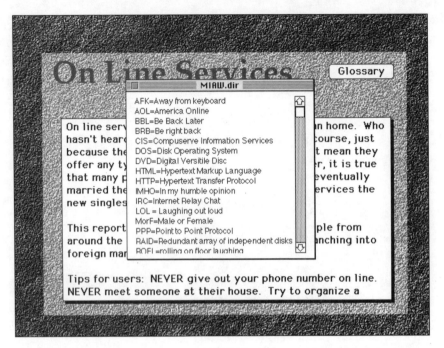

Figure 3.2 The host movie with **MIAW.dir** as a movie in a window.

Stop your movie.

Adding a Title to Your Movie in a Window

Open the script attached to the **Glossary** button. Add the following line as the first line of the handler:

```
set the title of window "MIAW.dir" to "Glossary"
```

Close the Script window and rewind your movie. Then play your movie and click the **Glossary** button. The title of the window has changed to Glossary. as shown in Figure 3.3.

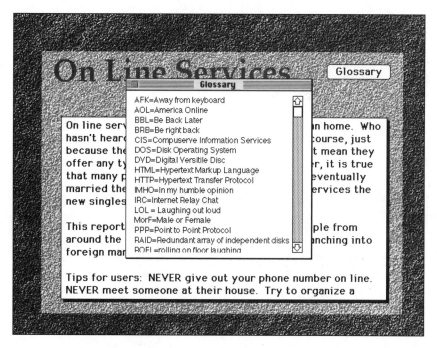

Figure 3.3 The movie in a window with the correct title displayed.

You need to take care of one last thing. Movies in a window love memory; they occupy a big chunk of it. To find out how much RAM they are using, find out how big the MIAW file is and add approximately 150 kilobytes for a rough approximation. That is why it is important to purge the movie in a window from memory when you no longer need it. In this case, the end user may need the glossary at any time, so purge it from memory when you quit out of the host movie. There is a primary event handler that will execute whenever the movie stops; it is called *on stopMovie*. The on stopMovie hander is executed whenever the movie is stopped, no matter what frame it is on. This primary event handler is a lot like the on startMovie handler you used in Chapter 2. Primary event handlers are usually located in movie scripts.

Stop your movie.

"Forgetting" a Movie in a Window

Open your movie script by choosing **Script** from the Window menu or pressing **Shift-command-U** on the Macintosh or **Shift -Ctrl-U** on Windows. Next type the following handler:

```
on stopMovie
      forget window "MIAW.dir"
end
```

The **Forget** command will remove the window from memory. Close the movie script.

Communicating between Movies

Host movies and movies in a window can "talk" to each other by sending commands, variables, or data back and forth. You will see how to accomplish this while programming the pull-down menu. (For instructions on how to create and install a pull-down menu, see Chapter 2.)

Open cast member 8. After `Open Notes|` type:

```
open window "Notes"
```

After `Close Notes|` type:

```
close window "notes"
```

To clear the Notes window we need to send a message to the movie in a window to tell it what to do. The Lingo you need to add after `clear notes|` is:

```
tell window "notes" to put "" into the field "text."
```

The **Tell** command passes commands from a host movie to a movie in a window.

The field "text" is the cast member in the notes movie created from an editable field cast member and named "text." `put "" into the field "text"` replaces the contents of the field with what is between the quotes. In this instance there is nothing between the quotes, so the text in the field cast member is simply erased.

You will also use the **Tell** command to print out your notes.

After `print notes|` add the following Lingo command (Figure 3.4):

```
tell window "notes" to printFrom 2,2
```

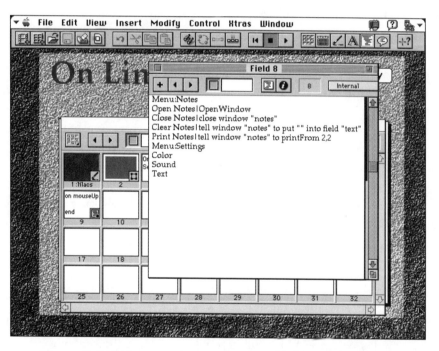

Figure 3.4 Field cast member 8 with Lingo added to pull-down menu.

The **printFrom** command will print everything that is on the stage for the range of frames indicated. In this case, you are just printing frame 2.

If you are using **printFrom** to print text on the stage, make sure the text you are going to print is created in a Field window, not a Text window. The text in a Field window will print using fonts on the user's computer while text in a Text window will be bitmapped. In other words, the text in a Text window will be printed at the screen resolution (usually 72 dpi) rather than taking advantage of the full resolution of the printer (typically 300 dpi or better) as the text in a Field window does. There are alternative ways to print Director screens using *Xtras*. The Xtra "PrintOMatic Lite" by Electric Ink and gray matter design ships with Director 5.0. You may want to investigate using this Xtra when you need to print from within a Director movie. See chapter 10 for details.

1. Close the Field window. Rewind and play your movie.
2. Test your commands under the Notes menu.

The Notes movie is really named **Notes.dir** but when you open it, the title of the window is just Notes. The extension does not show in the title of the window because you did not use it in the Lingo code, open window "notes". If you had typed open window "notes.dir", then the extension would have shown up in the title bar of the window.

Even with the Notes window closed, the **Clear** and the **Print** options work. Even though the window is closed, it is still in memory. It will remain in memory until you use the **Forget** command.

The movies in a window that you have created so far are movable, resizable windows. There are actually many different windows you can create, including boxes without title bars, windows that are not resizable, windows that are unmovable, and a rounded-corner window. When you do not specify the kind of window you want, you get the movable, sizable window without a zoom box. If you want to change the type of window being displayed, you need to use the **windowType of window command.** Let's create a window that is a plain box with no title bar.

This is the window you would use when creating a customized dialog box. You will need to change your **Open window** command. Because you need to use more than one line of Lingo, you should use a user-defined handler. If you try to type more than one line of code in the field window containing the menu, the second line of code actually becomes a menu choice in the Notes menu.

Open cast member 8. After open window| change the code to read:

```
OpenWindow
```

We have just created a handler name. Next we need to create this customized handler in the movie script. Open your movie script (**Shift-command-U** on Macintosh or **Shift-Ctrl-U** on Windows). Add the following handler:

```
on openWindow
     set the windowType of window "Notes" to 2
     open window "notes"
end
```

Close your movie script and try your movie.

You should see a different-looking window. Some other window types follow:

Type #	Attributes
0	Movable sizable window without Zoom-box feature
1	Alert box or modal dialog box
2	Plain box with no title bar
4	Movable window without size box on the Mac or maximize/minimize boxes in windows
8	Standard document window
12	Zoomable, unresizable window
16	Rounded-corner window
49	What Apple calls a *windoid*, or a floating palette

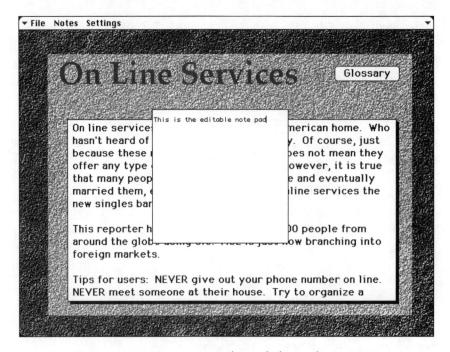

Figure 3.5 A Movie in a window with the windowType = 2

There is a window for just about anything you want to do. Types 1 and 2 are usually used as alert or dialog boxes. A modal dialog box must be closed before you continue. Type 8 is the typical window you see in a word processor. There are windoid-type windows in Director (Figure 3.6). They are usually used for Tools palettes. Be sure to pick an appropriate window type when using movies in a window. Check your *Using Lingo* book for more information on window types.

Last, we need to take care of a little "house-keeping." In order for the Notes window to come up empty whenever you restart the movie, we have to tell our host movie to forget the window. This will remove it from RAM and discard anything that the user might have typed there.

Open up your movie script. In the on stopMovie handler, add the line:

```
forget window "notes"
```

Figure 3.6 A windoid in Director.

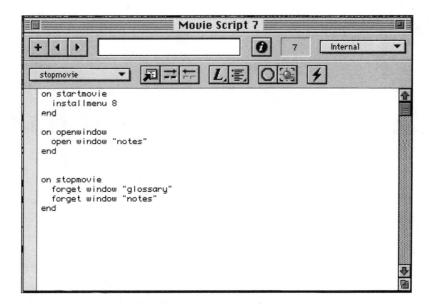

Figure 3.7 Your complete movie script.

Now that you can open two movies in a window, the Glossary and the Notes movies, give it a try. You see that both movies in a window can be open at the same time, but still only one window at a time can be active (Figure 3.8). Try different types of windows and a different number of windows open at the same time. Remember, however, that each additional movie in a window that is used eats up a considerable amount of memory.

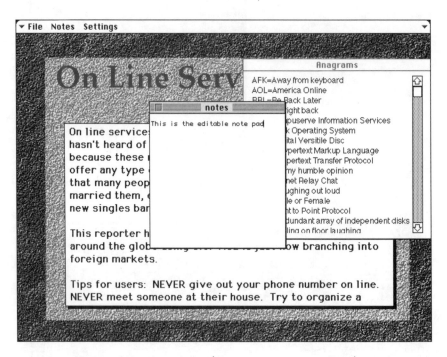

Figure 3.8 Host movie with two open movies in a window.

Summary

Movies in a window are the way to play more than one Director movie at a time. They are often used for customized dialog boxes, Help features, and to play QuickTime movies. You can open a movie in a window from a cast script, sprite script, or movie script. You can create your own title for the movie in a window. You can even customize it for each user, using the **Set the title of window** command. The host movie can send commands to the movie in a window using the **Tell** command. Also, the type of window is easily changed using the `windowType of window` Lingo so that you can create the appropriate look and functionality for your movies in a window.

CHAPTER 4

INTRODUCTION TO PUPPETS AND USER-DEFINED VARIABLES

Lingo included in this chapter:

```
puppetSprite
puppetSound
set the memberNum of sprite
random (number)
repeat while the mouseDown
global
updateStage
if...then
```

Puppets are an extremely powerful element in Director. They allow you to control sprites, sounds, tempos, and transitions with Lingo instead of using the score. Puppets are a bit more complicated than the Lingo we've seen up to this point. The Lingo is not harder, but the concepts behind the Lingo may be new to you. In order to give you some experience with puppets, you will build a dice game.

Getting Started

Open the Director movie **Ch4com.dir** on the CD that accompanies this book. Click on the **Roll** button and notice the dice "spin" and change color as long as the mouse button is held down. Let go of the mouse button and the dice stop, return to black on white, and the sum of the dice is displayed on the screen. Try the **Roll** button again. The dice come up in a random order every time you click the **Roll** button. Open the Cast window and look at the cast members used in the movie, as shown in Figure 4.1.

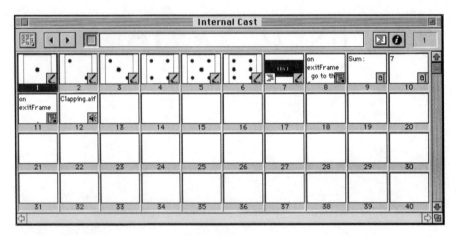

Figure 4.1 The Cast window for the Director movie **DiceCom.dir**.

There are six different cast members for the dice. When the **Roll** button is clicked, these members are randomly placed on the stage. Look at the score (Figure 4.2).

Only two frames are used. Of the six dice members, only members 1 and 2 are actually in the score. How are the other members showing up? To make the other members appear on the stage as they do, you need to use puppets and a randomizing feature. To show the sum of the dice, you will use global variables.

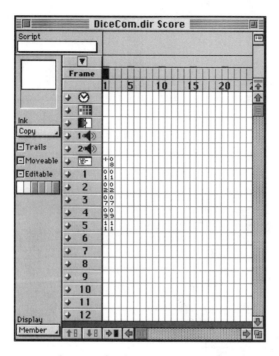

Figure 4.2 The score for the Director movie **DiceCom.dir**.

What are Puppets?

Sometimes we want to perform certain tasks in Director that are difficult if not impossible to do using the score alone. Take the dice, for example. Cast member 1 is in channel 1 of the score, yet when you click the **Roll** button, any one of the six dice cast members may appear on the stage. How can you put cast members 1 through 6 in the score and have them show up randomly when you click on the **Roll** button? What frames would you put the additional cast members in? It wouldn't be possible to do what you want to do if we could only use the score. Luckily, you can use Lingo. What you need to do is tell the sprites in channels 1 and 2 to show the cast member you indicate using Lingo commands instead of using the members in the score. In order to have sprites obey Lingo instead of the score, you must "puppet" them.

To understand what puppeting does, take the example of needing to take a taxi to the airport. You're sitting in your office and you say out loud "Come pick me up at 5:30 and drive me to the airport." You have given a command to the taxi driver, but unless the taxi driver is psychic, he has no idea what you just asked of him. He is not listening to you. Furthermore, he does not know he is supposed to be listening to you. You must first get his attention by calling him on the phone, then you can give him your command. Puppets work in a similar way. Although you can write code for your sprites to follow, they don't know to obey your command until you get their attention by puppeting them. A sprite is either a puppet or it is not. The default is that it is not a puppet. To make a sprite into a puppet, you use the Lingo command **puppetsprite TRUE**.

It's time to get some practical experience with puppets. Open the movie **Ch4.dir** and check out the score and cast member window. There are already the two dice on the stage. They are cast members 1 and 2. There is one frame script in frame 2, which is the command **go to the frame**.

In the score you have cast members 1 and 2, but for the dice to roll, we need to randomly show cast members 1 through 6.

Puppeting Sprites

In frame 1 of the script channel, open a Script window and type the following script:

```
on exitFrame
     puppetSprite 1, TRUE
     puppetSprite 2, TRUE
end
```

PuppetSprite 1, TRUE means to make the sprite located in channel 1 into a puppet, or in other words, tell the sprite in channel 1 to obey Lingo commands. The second line ensures that the sprite in channel 2 will also obey Lingo. Sprites are always referred to by the channel number in which they are located.

Close the Script window. Now you need to script the **Roll** button. You can make any graphic into a button by adding to it a cast member script or a sprite script. In this case, you always want the button to perform the same task so you'll do this with a cast member script. You will first just change one of the dice to show cast member 4 after the **Roll** button is clicked.

Select the **Roll** button in the Cast window and click on the **Script** button to open a Script window. Then type the following script in the mouseUp handler:

```
set the memberNum of sprite 1 to 4
```

This line tells Director to show cast member 4 in channel 1 instead of whatever cast member is in the score. MemberNum of sprite is a sprite property. Every sprite has several properties, including its location on the stage, its color, and its size. The word **Set** is a command. You can set properties or variables. For example, you are setting a property to a particular number.

The preceding Lingo code could also be written:
```
set the memberNum of sprite 1=4
```

When you see the word *the* in Lingo, it is usually referring to a property, whether it's a sprite property, a movie property, or a cast property.

Close the Script window, rewind, and play your movie.

Now that you are puppeting sprites in channel 1, it is *very important* to always rewind your movies and start from frame 1 or your movie will not execute the Lingo in the script channel of frame 1 and your sprites will not be puppeted, making the movie work incorrectly.

Click on the **Roll** button. The first die now shows up as a 4.

Now you will let Director randomly choose what cast member to show in channels 1 and 2.

Using Director's Random Feature

Open the script attached to the **Roll** button. Modify the mouseUp script to read as follows:

```
on mouseUp
      set the memberNum of sprite 1 to random (6)
      set the memberNum of sprite 2 to random (6)
end
```

Random is a Lingo function. Functions generally refer to a number, like in the case of *go to the frame*. The Frame function will return the frame number that the playback head is currently in. Random (6) tells Director to pick a number at random between 1 and 6. These numbers also happen to correspond to the cast member numbers of our dice. If the dice were somewhere else in the Cast Member window, say, cast members 10 through 15, then you would have to change your code so that you were still selecting the dice. For example, if the dice were cast members 10 through 15, the Lingo for sprite 1 would be set the memberNum of sprite 1 to random (6) + 9.

Close the Script window, rewind, and play your movie.

Remember to always close any Script windows that are open before playing your movie to ensure any script changes will take effect.

T I P

Now you should be getting two dice chosen at random every time you click on the **Roll** button.

Next you will change the script so the dice will change when you click on the **Roll** button instead of when you let go of the mouse button.

Open the script attached to the **Roll** button. Change the handler (shown in Figure 4.3) to read on mouseDown on the first line instead of on mouseUp.

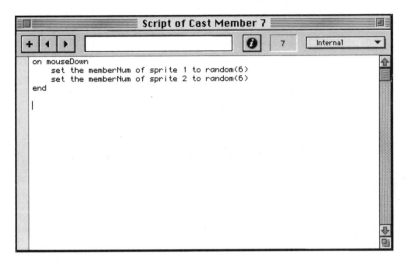

Figure 4.3 Your mouseDown handler.

Close the script. Play your movie and try your button. The dice do change when you click on the mouse, but they don't keep changing while you hold down the mouse button. Actually, you didn't ask them to yet. For that to happen, you need to add a few lines to your cast member script.

Using Repeat Loops

Open the script attached to the **Roll** button. Modify it to read as follows:

```
on mouseDown
    repeat while the mouseDown
        set the memberNum of sprite 1 to random (6)
        set the memberNum of sprite 2 to random (6)
    end repeat
end
```

Now your movie will keep changing the cast member numbers as long as you hold down the mouse button.

Repeat loops will continue to execute the lines of code between the `repeat` and `end repeat` lines as long as whatever condition following the command **repeat** is true. In this case, as long as the user is clicking on the **Roll** button, the cast members are changing. When the user releases the mouse button, the cast members stop changing.

Using Indents to Debug

Notice the indenting that takes place when using a repeat loop or an if-then statement. This indenting is another way to debug your scripts. The first thing you should do if a line is indenting improperly (see Figure 4.4) is hit the **Tab** key. This will tell Director to reformat the Script window, placing indents where they should be (see Figure 4.5). If you still have a line that is not indenting correctly, there is a problem with either that particular line or the line directly above it.

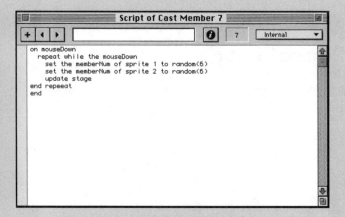

```
on mouseDown
  repeat while the mouseDown
      set the memberNum of sprite 1 to random(6)
      set the memberNum of sprite 2 to random(6)
      update stage
end repeeat
end
```

Figure 4.4 A Script with improper indenting.

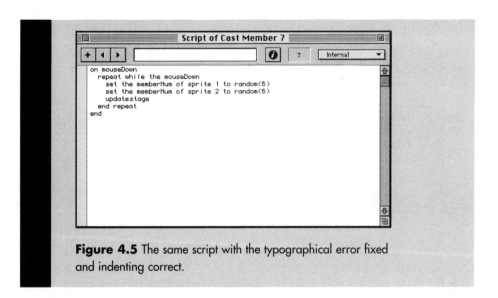

Figure 4.5 The same script with the typographical error fixed and indenting correct.

Close your script and try your movie. Is it working? Well, chances are it is working but Director isn't showing you the changes. You need to ask Director to keep refreshing or redrawing the screen so you can see the dice changing.

Open your cast member script (Figure 4.6) and add the following line before the `end repeat` line:

```
updateStage
```

`UpdateStage` tells Director to redraw the stage so that you can see the changes that are taking place.

Close the Script window and try playing your movie. You should have better results.

To have a little fun with the Random function, let's let Director randomly choose the color of the dice. The dice are actually constructed out of two colors: the dots, which are the foreground color, and the white box, which is the background color. To change the color of the box while leaving the dots black, you need to use the Lingo term, `the backColor of sprite`, which is another property. It refers to the background color of a 1-bit cast member. Using the backColor of sprite is equivalent to changing the background color using the background color chip in the Tools palette.

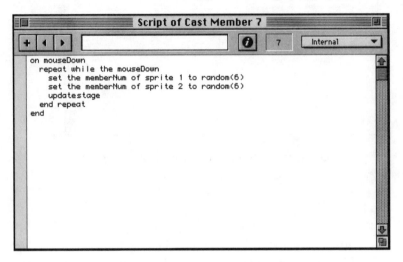

Figure 4.6 Your cast member script.

For you to be able to use the property the backColor of sprite, the sprite must be a puppet.

Using Colors with 1-Bit Cast Members

One-bit color means black and white, right? Usually it does, but Director is different. One of the truly great features of Director is its ability to apply colors to 1-bit cast members. Using 1-bit-color cast members makes your movie smaller, and small movies are the name of the game if you want to place your movies on the Internet. So, if you have a cast member that uses only one or two colors with no dithering, why not transform them into 1-bit-color cast members and use Director's Tools palette to color them? Follow these simple steps to create colored 1-bit cast members.

First, select the cast member you want to transform in the Cast window. Select **Transform Bitmap** from the Modify menu. Choose **1-bit-form color depth and remap colors** (Figure 4.7). Director will warn you that you cannot undo this operation. Click **OK**. Your cast member is now black.

Figure 4.7 Message window for **Transform Bitmap**.

Next, select **Tools** from the Window menu. Select the sprite that uses the 1-bit cast member and use the foreground color chip in the Tools palette (see Figure 4.8) to change the 1-bit color depth cast member to any of the 256 colors available. And there you have it! A 1-bit-color cast member! Remember, this technique is great when you are creating Shockwave movies for the Internet because it will make your movie smaller, requiring less download time.

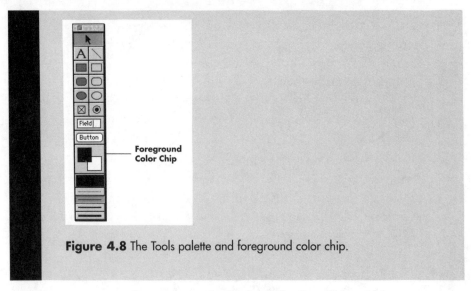

Figure 4.8 The Tools palette and foreground color chip.

Open your cast member script and add the following lines within your repeat loop:

```
set the backColor of sprite 1 to random (255) - 1
set the backColor of sprite 2 to random (255) - 1
```

As you may already know, Director works best with your monitor set to **8-bit color depth** or **256 colors**. Each color is assigned a number from 0 to 255; see, for example, Figure 4.9.

Random (255) will give you colors 1 through 255, with 255 being black. This does not include white, which has the color number 0, but it does include black, which isn't particularly useful in this case. You can eliminate black and include white by adding -1 to our code, so now we are using colors 0 through 254.

Now, try your movie.

There are several colors that are so dark that it is hard to see the dots on the dice, so you will set the background color of the dice to **white** when the dice stop rolling. For this you will add a mouseUp script.

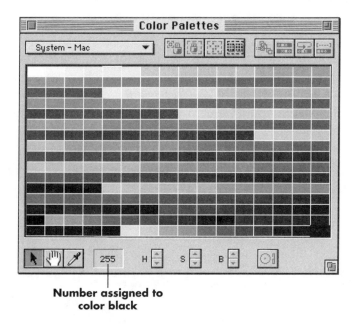

**Number assigned to
color black**

Figure 4.9 Color palette and color number.

Open your cast script and add the following handler:

```
on mouseUp
    set the backColor of sprite 1 to 0
    set the backColor of sprite 2 to 0
end
```

How does your movie look now?

Next we want to add the total of the dice. The reason we can do this fairly easily is because the number on the die is the same as the cast member number. Although we could add the total of the dice without customized variables, we will use both local and global variables.

What is a Variable?

A *variable* is nothing more than something that holds a value for you; this value can be a number, a word, or logical (true or false). The classic example is to think of a variable like a cup. At one instance the cup can hold orange juice. Later it can hold coffee. Next it might hold thumb tacks. The cup is a container for a number of different things. A variable works the same way. It may hold a number, or a name, or the condition TRUE. You could also think of a variable like a piece of paper. You might need to write down a phone number on the paper. Later you may need to write down a name to remember on the paper, later still maybe an address. You can re-use the paper to hold information for use later.

Creating User-Defined Variables

There are two easy ways to create and use your own variables. Both ways are equivalent, with neither way being better than the other. The following is an example:

```
put TRUE into paper
set paper = TRUE
```

The word *paper* here is our user-defined variable. A user-defined variable can be named anything you want except a Lingo term and cannot start with a number. Also, the name of the user-defined variable can be made out of several words, as long as you remove the spaces from between those words.

The first thing you will do is capture the final value of the cast member number of sprites 1 and 2 and place them in a user-defined variable so that you can add them together. We will use the variable names Dice1 and Dice2.

Open the cast member script and add the following lines after the end repeat line:

```
put the memberNum of sprite 1 into Dice1
put the memberNum of sprite 2 into Dice2
```

The preceding two lines could have also been written:
```
set Dice1 = the memberNum of sprite 1
set Dice2 = the memberNum of sprite 2
```

N O T E

To make sure that these variables are working, you will use the trace feature in the Message window.

Close your Script window and open the Message window. Click the **Trace** button in the Message tool bar. This turns on the trace feature. Figure 4.10 shows examples of the Message window and the **Trace** button.

Figure 4.10 Message window and **Trace** button.

Play your movie and click on your **Roll** button. Stop the movie. Scroll up in the Message window until you see your variables Dice1 and Dice2. Check out the values attached to your variables in the Message window and the actual dice shown on stage (Figure 4.11). These numbers should be the same. So now we are successfully capturing a value and storing it in our own customized variable. We need to add together those variables. We are going to use the variable "sum" to store the added value so that we can later display it on the screen.

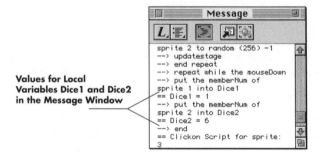

Values for Local Variables Dice1 and Dice2 in the Message Window

Figure 4.11 Locating variables in the Message window.

Once you have verified that your variables are capturing the right values, turn the trace feature off then close the message window.

If you do not turn the trace feature off and play your movie, your movie will be slowed down considerably. Even if the message window is closed, the trace feature is still active until you turn the trace off.

NOTE

The Message Window

The Message window is extremely helpful for both debugging and learning Lingo. The tool bar in the Message window has some invaluable features to help you learn Lingo (refer to Figure 4.12).

Figure 4.12 The Message tool bar and its features.

When learning Lingo, it is sometimes difficult to know the syntax of this new language. However, you can use the **Alphabetical Lingo** tool to select the Lingo you need. The correct syntax for the Lingo term is also shown. For example, if you look for the Lingo element stageColor under the letter *S* you will see that the correct term is *the stageColor*.

An ever better way to learn Lingo is to use the **Categorized Lingo** tool. Learning Lingo with the **Categorized Lingo** tool will help you learn a variety of terms that you might not otherwise be exposed to. Also, you may have a task at hand but not know how to go about executing it. For example, if you are interested in reducing your movie size or speeding up your movie, you can explore the Lingo elements under the Memory Management category (see Figure 4.13).

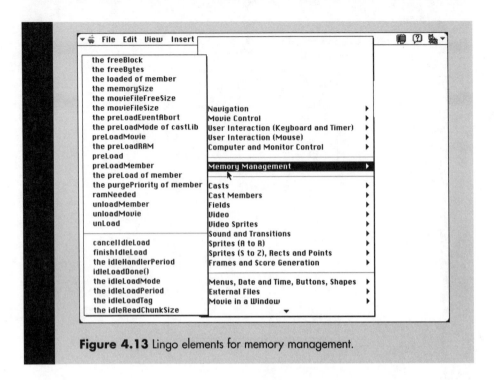

Figure 4.13 Lingo elements for memory management.

Open your cast member script and add the following line after the word `Dice2`:

```
set sum=dice1 + dice2
```

Again, you can track what is being stored in `sum` in the Message window.

Local Variables versus Global Variables

The sum will be displayed after the user lets go of the mouse button. Therefore you want to display the sum on mouseUp. The variables you have created up to this point are local variables. As soon as the playback head leaves the handler in which the variables were created, they are discarded. If you try to use the variable `sum` in your mouseUp handler, you will get the script error `variable used before assigned a value`. What you want to do is capture the value of sum in one handler and display it in another. You need to use a global variable. A *global variable* is a variable that will keep its value after the playback head has left a handler so that you can use the same variable and its assigned value in other handlers. To make a variable global, you need to declare it as a global variable in the first line in a Script window where the global variable is being used. Often global variables start with the letter *g* so that you can tell at a glance that it's a global variable.

Open your cast member script. At the top of the window, type **global gSum** and change the variable sum to gSum so that your entire handler looks like the following:

```
global gSum

on mouseDown
    repeat while the mouseDown
        set the memberNum of sprite 1 to random(6)
        set the memberNum of sprite 2 to random(6)
        updateStage
    end repeat
    set the backColor of sprite 1 to random (255) -1
    set the backColor of sprite 2 to random (255) -1
    put the memberNum of sprite 1 into Dice1
    put the memberNum of sprite 2 into Dice2
    set gSum = Dice1 + Dice2
end
```

Contrary to popular belief, you do not need the global declaration line in every handler for which you are using the global variable. You only need the global declaration line once at the top of a Script window in which at least one of the handlers contains the global variable.

Now you can use the variable gSum in the mouseUp handler. However, you still need a way to display the result on the stage. You can use a field cast member and Lingo to do this.

Choose **Field** from the Window menu. In the text field, place a few spaces so Director will not automatically throw away the empty field.

Name this cast member **readout**. It is very important to name this cast member because you are going to use its name in Lingo. Figure 4.15 demonstrates naming a cast member.

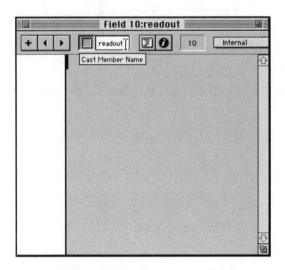

Figure 4.15 Naming a cast member.

From the Cast window, select the field and drag it onto the stage next to the word sum.

In your mouseUp handler (Figure 4.16), before the word end, type the following line of code:

```
put gSum into field "readout."
```

Close the Script window and try your movie. You should now get the sum displaying on the stage.

What if you wanted a sound to play if the dice total was 7? How could you put that in the score? It would take some very creative ideas to get that done, if it could be accomplished at all! Once again, puppets come to your aid, but this time with puppetSound.

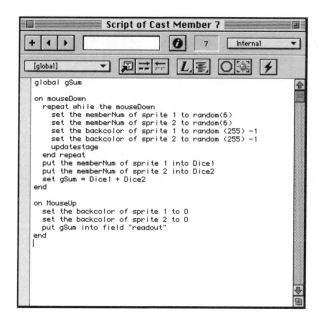

Figure 4.16 Your mouseUp handler.

Open your **Roll** button cast member script and modify your mouseUp handler to read as follows:

```
on mouseUp
    set the backColor of sprite 1 to 0
    set the backColor of sprite 2 to 0
    put gSum into field "readout"
    if gSum = 7 then
        puppetSound "clapping.aif"
    end if
end
```

Just like every repeat loop needs to end with `end repeat`, every `if` statement needs an `end if` statement.

If-Then-Else Statements

In an *if-end if* statement, there is a condition and one or more statements that are executed if the condition is true. If the condition is not true, you may also have one or more statements that are executed. Take, for example, when it rains. If it is raining, you will drive to work; otherwise, you will walk. If you wrote this example in Lingo, it would look like this:

```
if raining = TRUE then
     drive to work
else
     walk
end if
```

Notice the structure of the if-then statement. The statement executes if the condition on a separate line is true. The word *else* is on its own line with the statement that executes if the condition on its own line is false. The last line of this if-then-else is always *end if*. The end if tells the playback head that the statements attached to the if-then-else are finished.

The **puppetSound** command takes over sound channel 1. Because of this, if you had a sound playing in sound channel 1, that sound would be turned off when the puppetSound started playing, because what we are saying in essence here is "don't play whatever sound is in the score's sound channel 1, play what I'm telling you to play with Lingo." If you want another sound to play while the puppetSound is playing, use sound channel 2.

NOTE

To get your movie to play what is in sound channel 1 after a puppetSound has played, you need to issue the **puppetSound 0** command to give back control to the score.

Close the Script window. and rewind and play your movie. You are well on your way to creating a Las Vegas–type craps game!

Summary

There are times when you need to accomplish certain tasks that would be difficult if not impossible to do in the score. Examples of these are changing cast members or playing a sound that is not in the score on a **mouseDown** command. In these cases, you need to use puppets. Puppets follow commands you issue using Lingo instead of what is in the score. For sprites to follow your Lingo commands, we first need to puppet them so that they know when to follow Lingo and when to follow the score.

User-defined variables, or customized variables, are used to hold information. You can perform mathematical tasks on variables, display them, or store information received from the user in them, among other things. Variables used in a handler and then discarded are *local variables*, while variables used in more than one handler need to be *global variables*. To create a global variable, you need to type the word **global** and the name of the variable or variables as the first line in the Script window in which the global variable is used.

CHAPTER 5

USING PUPPETS TO CREATE A BUTTON HANDLER

Lingo included in this chapter:

```
puppetSprite
puppetSound
rollOver
the memberNum of sprite
repeat while the mouseDown
```

You have seen puppets in Chapter 4, but there are a lot more issues you need to address when using puppets. Most often, when you use puppets, you only use them for a short time, then you turn the puppets off when you no longer need them. Also, as a multimedia developer, you need to make sure your elements work according to human interface guidelines. When you use Director's **Button** tool, the button created already follows these guidelines. When you use your own graphic for a button, however, you need to script your buttons to work in accordance with the human interface guidelines. In this chapter, you will learn when to use puppets and when to turn them off and you'll create custom buttons that work according to human interface guidelines.

At the end of this chapter, you will have created a basic button handler. Don't let the name fool you; although it is considered a basic handler, it contains many different parts that when put together create a very powerful handler that anyone who considers themselves a Lingo programmer must know.

Open and play the movie **Ch5Com.dir**. Notice the movie pauses on frame 2. Click the top button. The movie branches to a QuickTime movie of the earth. Click the **Return** button then click the second button on the main screen. Notice that when you clicked the button, it changed to a "down state," then returned to its original form. The movie branches to an animation of the solar system. Go back to the main screen. Hold down the mouse button on the top button. Then, with the mouse button held down, drag the pointer off the button, then let go of the mouse button. As soon as the pointer is no longer on the button while the mouse button is held down, the button returns to its original image, or its "up state." When you let go of the mouse button this time, you did not branch to the animation. You only branch to the animation when your pointer is still on the button after you let go of the mouse button. All of these behaviors follow the human interface guidelines.

Human Interface Guidelines

In most well-programmed computer applications, a button on the screen will change slightly in some way when it is clicked to give the user visual feedback that he or she has selected that button. When the user is no longer holding down the mouse button, the button on the screen will return to its original state before further action is taken. The button's original graphic is called the *up state* and the graphic used for the visual feedback is called the *down state*. Most often, multimedia developers will use the same graphic for the down state but change it in some small way, whether that is to rotate the button 180°, darken or lighten parts of it, or even move the button a couple of pixels down the stage.

What if the user realizes they have clicked the button in error? How many times have you chosen the **Print** button and then remembered that the printer is either disconnected or turned off? What do you do? Most likely, after clicking the **Print** button, you drag the pointer off the **Print** button, then let go of the mouse button. That way, you know the **Print** command has not been activated. A well-programmed button will only trigger some other action if the user has both clicked on the button and kept the pointer on the button when he or she lets go of the mouse button. These things seem to happen all by themselves, but a lot of thought and programming actually take place in order for these buttons to work seamlessly. In this chapter, you will learn the magic behind these buttons.

Every platform has its own set of human interface guidelines that varies slightly from one operating system to another. Make sure to investigate the particular human interface guidelines for the platform(s) for which you are developing.

N O T E

Getting Started

Open the movie **ch5.dir**. Notice that the buttons take up only two frames. The script in frame 2 of the script channel is go to the frame. The rest of the score has the animation (Figure 5.1).

When a button is clicked, you want it to change in some way, to indicate to the user that they have indeed clicked the button, and then have the button return to its normal state. In this case, you want the button to change to cast member 1, the "button down" cast member, and then return back to cast member 2. Where would you put cast member 1 in the score? How do you know when the user has selected the button? You can see that it would be difficult to do these two tasks in the score. It's puppets to the rescue! Let's just take care of the first button located in channel 2 of the score. First, you need to tell Director that the button is going to obey Lingo instead of the score.

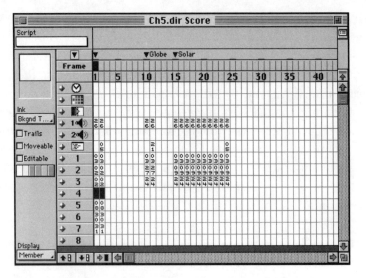

Figure 5.1 The score for the movie **ch5.dir**.

Puppeting a Sprite

Open a Script window in frame 1 of the script channel and type the following:

```
puppetSprite 2, TRUE
```

You have just told Director that the sprite in channel 2 is going to obey Lingo.

Using a Sprite Script to Switch Cast Members

Next, you need to tell the button what to do when someone clicks on it. So far you have used member scripts to do this, but this time is different. We have one graphic that is used for two separate tasks. Cast member 2 is not always doing the exact same thing. You need to use a sprite script. In this way, you can script the same graphic to do two different things, depending on which instance of the button the user clicks on.

Who's on First?

In a single frame you can have frame scripts, sprite scripts, and cast scripts; which one is being executed? Lingo has a strict hierarchy to follow. If you have all three types of scripts in a single frame, the frame script is usually first activated. If, in that same frame, you click on a sprite that has a cast script attached to it, the cast script overrides the frame script. If you have a sprite that has a cast script attached to the cast member it is created from *and* a sprite script attached to it, the sprite script will override the cast script. In this way, you can have a cast script on a button and have it execute the same way all the time. However, if you need one particular instance of that cast member to act differently, place a sprite script on that particular instance. In this way, you can have the button behave as you need it to and cut down on programming at the same time.

Select **frame 2** of channel 2. Click the **Script Preview** area. A Script window opens. It looks just like a cast member script with the handler "on mouseUp" in it. "On mouseUp" means after the mouse button has been clicked and released. Whatever we type here will take effect after the user has clicked the button.

Type the following handler:

```
set the memberNum of sprite 2 to 1
```

You have just told the sprite in channel 2 to display cast member 1 after the user clicks the button in channel 2.

Close the Script window, then rewind your movie. Play your movie and click the top button.

You're off to a good start! The button changes to its down state after you click on it but does not return to its up state afterward. What you really want to happen is for the down state of the button to show as soon as you click on the button and for the up state to show after you click the button. You will now change your sprite script to make this work.

Stop your movie and save it.

Make sure your movie is not playing while you are making changes. In most instances, Director will not let you make changes if the movie is playing.

T I P

1. Open the sprite script in frame 2, channel 2.

2. Change *on mouseUp* to read *on mouseDown*.

3. Add the following handler after your mouseDown handler (Figure 5.2 shows your revised sprite script):

```
on mouseUp
     set the memberNum of sprite 2 to 2
end
```

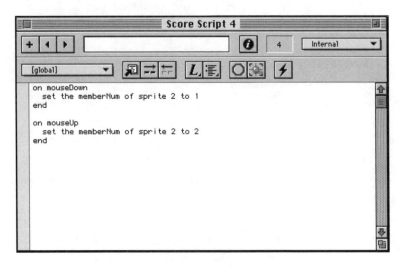

Figure 5.2 Your revised sprite script.

Even though the mouseDown event happens first, we could have placed the mouseUp handler before it in the Script window. The order of the handlers in the window does not matter.

NOTE

Close the Script window and rewind and play your movie. Now try your button. It appears to be working, but it is not branching anywhere. You want this first button to branch to the "Globe" QuickTime movie. You need to add a line to the *mouseUp* handler. Stop your movie.

Branching with a Sprite Script

Open the sprite script located in frame 2, channel 2 and add a line to the mouseUp handler to make your handler look like this:

```
on mouseUp
     set the memberNum of sprite 2 to 2
     go to "globe"
end
```

Close the Script window and rewind and play your movie. Now click the top button. What happens? The top button remains on the stage, and the QuickTime movie doesn't play. Earlier, you told the sprite in channel 2 to obey Lingo instead of what's in the score. That is what is happening now. In Lingo, you told Director to show cast member number 2 in channel 2. Now you see that sometimes you must tell Director to stop doing what you asked it to do in Lingo and to go back to the score. To do that, you need to turn off your puppet by declaring the puppet to be FALSE. This command needs to be issued before the button branches to the QuickTime movie. Stop your movie.

Turning Off a Puppet

Open the sprite script located in frame 2, channel 2. Before the go to line, add the following to turn off the puppet (Figure 5.3):

```
PuppetSprite 2, FALSE
```

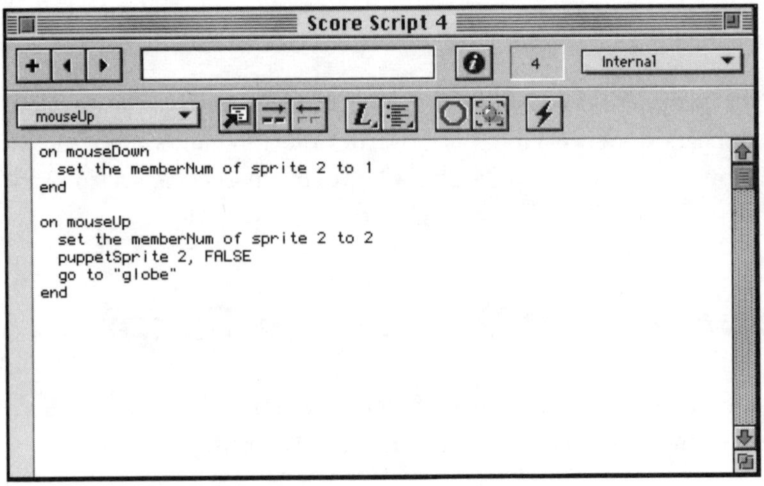

```
on mouseDown
  set the memberNum of sprite 2 to 1
end

on mouseUp
  set the memberNum of sprite 2 to 2
  puppetSprite 2, FALSE
  go to "globe"
end
```

Figure 5.3 Turning off a puppet in the sprite script.

Close the Script window. Rewind and play your movie and then try your button again. You should get much better results! Now stop your movie.

Everything looks great so far. Now you must consider more human interface guidelines. What happens if you click the button, then drag your pointer off of it? What if you drag off of it and then let go of the mouse button? When you drag the pointer off of it, the button should return to its up state. When you let go of the mouse button, it should not branch to the QuickTime movie. Both of these things are not working properly. You are going to need to add more Lingo to your sprite script.

Integrating Human Interface Guidelines

Open the sprite script located in frame 2, channel 2. You will use a if-then-else statement to check whether the pointer is on or off the sprite.

Change your handler to look like this:

```
on mouseDown
     if rollOver (2) = TRUE then
          set the memberNum of sprite 2 to 1
     else
          set the memberNum of sprite 2 to 2
     end if
end
```

The line that starts with `if rollOver` states that if the pointer is on sprite 2, then set sprite 2 to display cast member 1. RollOver is a function that indicates whether or not the pointer is over a sprite. RollOver is TRUE if the pointer is on the sprite and FALSE if the pointer is not on the sprite.

This script does work once as soon as the user clicks on the button. However, we want this script to keep executing for as long as the user holds down the mouse button. That way, if the user clicks the button and then decides he or she didn't want to click it, he or she can drag off of the button and then let go of the mouse button.

To make the script keep executing, add the following bold lines:

```
on mouseDown
     repeat while the mouseDown
          if rollOver (2) = TRUE then
               set the memberNum of sprite 2 to 1
          else
               set the memberNum of sprite 2 to 2
          end if
     end repeat
end
```

Now when your movie is playing and you click the button, Director will constantly check the location of the pointer and update the button state based on the position of the pointer.

There is one more piece of Lingo you need to add. You need to tell Director to keep showing you the changes that are taking place on the stage. You need to add the command **updateStage** to your handler before `end repeat`; your complete handler should look like this:

```
on mouseDown
     repeat while the mouseDown
          if rollOver (2) = TRUE then
               set the memberNum of sprite 2 to 1
          else
               set the memberNum of sprite 2 to 2
          end if
          updateStage
     end repeat
end
```

Close the Script window.

If you are getting a script error, look at your script. Are you getting the proper indenting for the `if-then-else` statement and the `repeat` loop? If so, check your spelling carefully. Most script errors are simple spelling mistakes. Also, make sure that you typed **updateStage** as one word.

1. Rewind and play your movie.
2. Click down on the button.
3. Drag the pointer off of the button. The button should now be in its up state.
4. Drag the pointer back on the button. The button returns to its down state.
5. Drag off of the button again and let go of the mouse button.

You are still branching to the movie even though the pointer was not on the button when you let go. This is a problem that is easily fixed. You need to branch only if the pointer is still on the button. Using the rollOver function will help you do that.

1. Stop your movie.
2. Open the sprite script located at frame 2, channel 2.
3. Change the mouseUp handler to match the following:

```
on mouseUp
     if rollOver (2) then
          set the memberNum of sprite 2 to 2
          puppetSprite 2, FALSE
          go to "globe"
     else
          exit
     end if
end
```

Now, if the pointer is still located on your button, the movie branches to the globe QuickTime movie. If the pointer is not on sprite 2, then the playback head will exit the handler and not branch anywhere.

Using Comments

In every scripting language, you can add lines to your script that the computer will not read. You may have heard them referred to as remarks in some programming environments. In Lingo, they are called *comments*. A comment is prefaced by a double dash (--). You have already seen comments in the Message window (Figure 5.4).

Figure 5.4 The Message window with comments.

Comments are handy in two ways. One is that you can add lines in a script that describe what particular handlers or lines of Lingo are doing, like in the movie script of the **ch5com.dir** movie. Notice that the commented lines are in red so it is easy to spot what lines are code and what are lines of description. These comment lines are colored using the color chip in the Tools palette.

It is easy to add a comment. You can either type two dashes or use the button in the Script Window tool bar to add a comment (see Figure 5.5, the **Comment** button).

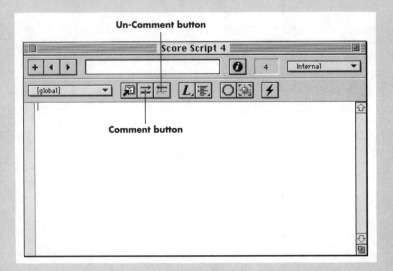

Figure 5.5 The **Comment** button in the Script window.

The other use of comments is that you can "comment out" lines of code and then see how your program works without them. The alternative to this would be removing lines of code completely to see how your program works without them and then retyping them into your program. If you are having trouble understanding what a particular line of Lingo is doing in this chapter, comment it out, play your movie, and see the difference.

You now have one button working correctly; it's time to tackle the second button. It would be great if you could just attach the sprite script you just wrote to the other button, but that won't work. Look at your sprite script. You have scripted it to react to elements located in a particular channel. It will only work for the sprite in channel 2. This script is too specific to work in another place. You would have to place a similar script on the sprite in channel 3 to make the two buttons work correctly.

In this example, you only have two buttons. Imagine if you had 30 buttons that all needed to work according to human interface guidelines. Would you want to create 30 long sprite scripts to make them work? Of course not. There is a way to use one script with all 30 buttons. Place the sprite script in the movie script, then make it more generic so it will work with any number of buttons. That is what you are going to do now.

Creating User-Defined Handlers in the Movie Script

Open your sprite script and cut it and paste it in the movie script. You can open your movie script by selecting **Script** from the Window menu.

The names of handlers in the movie script for the most part need to be user-defined names that are not part of Lingo. You will never see the handler names *on mouseUp*, *on mouseDown*, *on exitFrame*, or *on enterFrame* in the movie script. You need to rename the handlers you just pasted into the movie script. The easiest thing to do is to name them *on down* and *on up*. Do this now.

You now need to make sure the handlers are not channel- or sprite-specific. The sprite number is going to change depending on what channel the sprite is in. Because the sprite number is going to change, you can place a variable in your script wherever the script refers to a particular sprite. This is a user-defined variable, not a Lingo term. In this example, use the variable *ChanNum*, which stands for channel number. Now replace all instances of a sprite number with the user-defined variable ChanNum in your up and down handlers. Your handlers will look like the following:

```
on Down
 repeat while the mouseDown
  if rollOver (ChanNum) = TRUE then
   set the memberNum of sprite ChanNum to 1
  else
   set the memberNum of sprite ChanNum to 2
  end if
  updateStage
 end repeat
end

on Up
 if rollOver (ChanNum) then
  set the memberNum of sprite ChanNum to 2
  puppetsprite ChanNum, FALSE
  go to "globe"
 else
  exit
 end if
end
```

Type the variable name once, then copy and paste it wherever you need it. This will cut down on typing mistakes in your handlers.

T I P

If you try to close the movie script window now, you will get the error vari-able used before assigned a value. The variable it is referring to is chanNum. Director can't find a value for it and assumes it is an error. You can't give it a value here because the value will be changing. In this case, you need to tell Director that chanNum is an argument. An *argument* is simply a place holder that lets you pass values to a handler.

To tell Director that chanNum is an argument, place it after the handler name so the first lines of your handlers looks like this:

```
on down chanNum
   ...

on up chanNum
   ...
```

It is possible to have more than one argument being passed to a handler. In that case, separate the arguments with commas.

Now you have your handlers in the movie script. Next, you need to tell Director when to execute those handlers, and you also need to give values to your arguments. You will do these two things with a sprite script.

Calling Handlers

Open the sprite script at frame 2, channel 2. Enter the following two handlers:

```
on mouseDown
        down 2
end

on mouseUp
        up 2
end
```

Now when the user clicks the button, the mouseDown handler is activated. The playback head reads the line, *down 2*, which is not part of Lingo. The playback head assumes it's a user-defined handler and goes to the movie script to look for a handler named Down and a place to put the number 2. When it finds the handler *down*, it also finds the argument name chanNum. The playback head then executes the *down* handler, replacing *chanNum* with the numeric value 2. Remember that the number 2 stands for the sprite located in channel 2.

1. Close the Script window.
2. Save your movie.
3. Rewind and play your movie.

It should play just like it did before you created your handlers in the movie script. It's easy now to script the second button. You will use another sprite script. Choose the cell located at **frame 2, channel 3**. Click the **Script Preview** area to open a Script window. Now add the following handler:

```
on mouseDown
      down 3
end

on mouseUp
      up 3
end
```

What does the *3* stand for? It's the channel that the second button is in.

Before the second button will work, you need to make it a puppet.

1. Open a Script window in the script channel, frame 1.
2. Add the following line:

    ```
    puppetSprite 3, TRUE
    ```

3. Close the Script window. Rewind and play your movie.

What happens? You have buttons staying on the screen, **Return** buttons missing, and both buttons go to the same place in the score. Look at your movie script. In your *Up* handler you have the line `puppetsprite chanNum, FALSE`. You are only turning off one of the puppets. You still have one puppet always on. That is why you have a button remaining on the stage. When you click the top button, the handlers are executed, and the channel 2 puppet is turned off, returning control to the score for channel 2. The QuickTime movie plays, but the **Return** button in channel 3 does not show. Channel 3 is still puppeted, taking control away from the score. You need to make sure all puppets are turned off once a button is clicked.

Open your movie script. Remove `puppetSprite chanNum, FALSE`. Replace it with the following two lines:

```
puppetSprite 2, FALSE
puppetSprite 3, FALSE
```

Now you can tackle the branching problem. In your *up* handler, you have the line `go to "globe"`, so both buttons are branching to the same place. You need to make the location an argument so that you can tell the movie where to branch with each button. Again, this argument is a user-defined variable. Don't forget to add this argument to the first line of the handler where it is used.

Change your *up* handler so that it looks like this:

```
on Up chanNum, animation
    if rollOver (chanNum) then
        set the memberNum of sprite chanNum to 2
        puppetsprite 2, FALSE
        puppetsprite 3, FALSE
        go to animation
    else
        exit
    end if
end
```

Now you need to add the destination of your buttons to their respective sprite handlers. Open the sprite script located at frame 2, channel 2. Change your *mouseUp* handler to look like this:

```
on mouseUp
    up 2, "Globe"
end
```

Don't forget the quotation marks around the label name *Globe*.

Close the Script window. Open the sprite script located at frame 2, channel 3. Add the destination to this *mouseUp* handler as well:

```
on mouseUp
    up 3, "solar"
end
```

Close the Script window. Rewind and play your movie. Both buttons work now!

There is one last thing to incorporate in your button handler: sound. We will add a sound when someone clicks the button.

Adding a Button Sound

Open your movie script. In the *down* handler, add the *puppetSound* line of code as the first line of the handler:

```
on Down chanNum
    puppetSound "click.aif"
    repeat while the mouseDown
        if rollOver (chanNum) = TRUE then
            set the memberNum of sprite chanNum to 1
        else
            set the memberNum of sprite chanNum to 2
        end if
        updateStage
    end repeat
end
```

If you are creating a multimedia presentation that needs to run on both the Macintosh and Windows platforms, use AIFF sound files since they work on both platforms.

T I P

Close the movie script. Rewind and play your movie. What happened to your music? It no longer plays. That is because when you use a puppet sound, the puppetSound is played instead of what is in sound channel 1. The **puppetSound** command tells Director "play the sound I tell you to play in Lingo, not what is in sound channel 1 of the score." To get back your sound, you need to turn off the puppetSound when you no longer need it. To turn off the puppetSound and give control back to the score, you need to issue the command **puppetSound 0**.

Turning Off a PuppetSound

Stop your movie and open your movie script. In the *up* handler, you need to add the command **puppetSound 0** in two places:

```
on Up chanNum, where
     if rollOver (chanNum) then
          set the memberNum of sprite chanNum to 2
          puppetsprite 2, FALSE
          puppetsprite 3, FALSE
          puppetSound 0
          go to where
     else
          puppetSound 0
          exit
     end if
end
```

You puppeted the sound in the *down* handler and are turning it off in the *up* handler. However, there are two possible outcomes when the user lets go of the mouse button: Either the pointer is on the button or it's not. If it is, you need to turn off the puppetSound before the branching. If the pointer is not on the button, you still need to turn off the puppetSound before the playback head exits the handler or the music will not be heard. Close the movie script. Rewind and play your movie. Everything works!

And there you have it: the basic button handler. One of the great things about creating a handler like this is that once you create it, you can cut and paste it wherever you need it. You might even want to start your own Lingo script library to store all your new scripts.

Summary

Creating buttons out of your own graphics is not difficult, if you don't care about following human interface guidelines. Creating a button that works according to these guidelines is more complex, but the results are worth it. Now your buttons work as the end user assumes they will.

You now have separate graphics for the up and down states of your button that switch when the user clicks it. The graphics are put in place using puppets instead of the score. You learned when to turn off a puppet and return control to the score. Also, the buttons only branch to other parts of the score if the user mouses down and up on the button. If the user mouses down on the button but drags off the button and then lets go of the mouse button, the button on the stage will not branch to further animation. You added a sound to your button using a puppetSound. The puppetSound was turned off with Lingo when it was no longer needed.

Don't forget that you also used the movie script to hold the up and down handlers so that you could access the same script for both buttons. You added arguments to send specific information to those handlers in the movie script so they would work properly for both buttons. You will soon find out that it is not uncommon to have eight or ten buttons on the screen at once. Using the movie script to store your handlers lets you create a script once and use it in many different places by calling it whenever you need it.

CHAPTER 6

ROLLOVERS

Lingo included in this chapter:

```
the visible of sprite
the ink of sprite
rollOver ()
```

You used rollOvers in Chapter 5 in conjunction with creating a button handler, but sometimes you want something to happen when the user places the cursor over a button or particular place on the stage. This may be for a sprite to move, a new movie to start, a button to highlight, or for a pop-up label to appear next to a tool, giving the user information about the particular tool, like you see in Director. All of these things can be done with rollOvers. In this chapter you, will use rollOvers for two tasks. First, you will use rollOvers to give your users visual feedback as to which buttons are active. Second, you will use rollOvers to show tool tips: When the user positions the mouse pointer over a button, a sprite will appear indicating what that button is for.

Getting Started

Open the movie **Ch6Com.dir** on the CD accompanying this book. Play the movie. Notice that when you place the cursor over one of the buttons on the right-hand side of the stage, the button changes from blue to yellow. When the cursor is no longer on the button, it changes back to blue. This type of rollOver gives your user visual feedback, indicating that a button is active. Try each button. They control the QuickTime movie. (You will learn how to script these buttons to control Digital Video in the next chapter.) If you place the cursor on one of the round buttons on the bottom of the stage, nothing happens. These buttons do not have a rollOver effect to them, indicating that they are not active.

Look at the score for this movie, as shown in Figure 6.1.

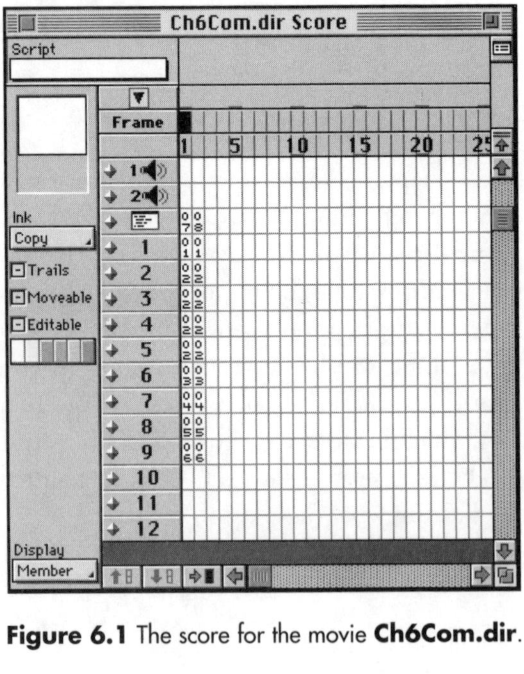

Figure 6.1 The score for the movie **Ch6Com.dir**.

You see that each button is a separate sprite. If you look in the frame script in frame 2 (Figure 6.2), you will see how the button is changing color. Set the ink of sprite 2 to 4 is changing the ink effect of the button from **Matte** to **Not Copy**.

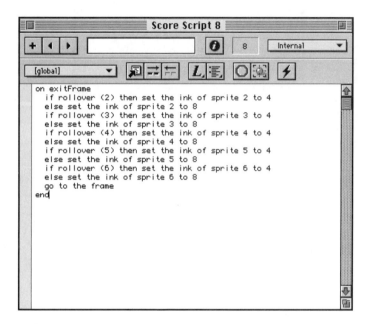

Figure 6.2 The frame script that creates rollOvers.

Open movie **Ch6.dir**. Notice that there is a script in the script channel in frame 2. It is go to the frame. The first thing we should do is puppet the buttons on the stage so that they will follow your Lingo commands instead of what is in the score (see Figure 6.3).

Figure 6.3 Puppeting buttons in the frame script.

Open a Script window at frame 1, script channel and type the following frame script:

```
repeat with x=2 to 5
    puppetSprite x, TRUE
end repeat
```

Remember that a repeat loop like this will puppet any number of sprites. In this particular case, it is puppeting the sprites located in Chapters 2 through 5, the buttons. Otherwise, the handler would look like the following:

```
on exitFrame
    puppetSprite 2, TRUE
    puppetSprite 3, TRUE
    puppetSprite 4, TRUE
    puppetSprite 5, TRUE
end
```

Imagine if you had to puppet 10 buttons. Using the repeat loop is easier and just as effective.

 If you want to use a repeat loop for puppeting, make sure the sprites you want to puppet are in adjacent channels of the score.

Close the Script window.

You will start by creating a rollOver for the top button. What do you need to happen? You need your movie to check continuously whether or not the cursor is on the button. In the last chapter, you only needed to check where the cursor was while the mouse button was being held down. Now you need to check the location of the cursor constantly. You can use the script in frame 2 of the script channel to help you do this. The Lingo go to the frame keeps the playback head in motion. You can check the rollOver in this script. It will continue to execute and check the location of the cursor.

Open the Script window located in the script channel in frame 2. Change the script to match the following:

```
on exitFrame
    if rollOver (2) then set the ink of sprite 2 to 4
    go to the frame
end
```

The button you are scripting the rollOver for is in channel 2 of the score. That is why you are setting the ink for sprite 2.

RollOver () is a function. Remember, functions return a value. RollOver returns a 1 if the cursor is over the sprite indicated within the parentheses. RollOver will return a 0 if the cursor is not over the sprite indicated. In Boolean logic, 1 stands for TRUE and 0 for FALSE. So, the preceding line translates to "if it is true that the cursor is on the sprite in channel 2, then set the ink effect of that sprite to **Not Copy**."

The preceding Lingo code could have been written:

```
on exitFrame
    if rollOver (2) = TRUE then
        set the ink of sprite 2 to 4
    end if
    go to the frame
end
```

If you have an if-then structure that has only one statement attached to it, you can write it in one line instead of two. With one-line if-then statements, you do not need the `end-if` statement. With the one-line if-then statement, when the condition expressed after the word *if* is true, then Lingo executes the statement that follows *then*. When the condition is not true, nothing happens unless you have an else statement. In that case, Lingo executes the statement that follows *else*.

The *ink of sprite* is a sprite property. All ink effects have a corresponding number, which can be found in your Lingo Dictionary. If you don't have your Lingo Dictionary handy, use the Message window. First, find an ink effect that you like by changing the ink effects on the particular sprite you are working with (Figure 6.4). Next, open the Message window. Type in the window:

```
put the ink of sprite x
```

The Message window will return a number. This is the number you need to use in conjunction with the ink of sprite. In this case, you are using **Not Copy** when the sprite is rolled over and **Matte** when the cursor is not on the sprite.

T I P   Although both **Background Transparent** and **Matte** ink effects will give you the same visual effect, Director will execute a bit faster with the **Matte** ink effect than with **Background Transparent**.

Figure 6.4 Finding the number corresponding to **Ink Effect Not Copy** with the Message window.

1. Close your Script window.

2. Rewind and play your movie.

3. Place your cursor over the top button. The button turns yellow.

4. Move the cursor off the button. The button remains yellow. You need to make sure the ink effect returns to **Matte** when the cursor is not on the sprite.

5. Stop your movie.

6. Open the frame script in frame 2.

7. Add an else statement:

```
on exitFrame
      if rollOver (2) then set the ink of sprite 2 to 4
      else set the ink of sprite 2 to 8
      go to the frame
end
```

8. Close the frame script, rewind, and play your movie.

Now the button changes color when you roll over it and returns to its original color when the cursor is no longer on it.

It's time to script the rest of the rollOvers. The other buttons are in channel 3, 4, and 5.

1. Stop your movie.

2. Open the script located in the script channel, frame 2.

3. Add the following **bold** lines to your exitFrame handler:

```
on exitFrame
        if rollOver (2) then set the ink of sprite 2 to 4
        else set the ink of sprite 2 to 8
        if rollOver (3) then set the ink of sprite 3 to 4
        else set the ink of sprite 3 to 8
        if rollOver (4) then set the ink of sprite 4 to 4
        else set the ink of sprite 4 to 8
        if rollOver (5) then set the ink of sprite 5 to 4
        else set the ink of sprite 5 to 8
        if rollOver (6) then set the ink of sprite 6 to 4
        else set the ink of sprite 6 to 8
        go to the frame
end
```

4. Close your Script window.

5. Rewind and play your movie. See what happens when you place the cursor on each of the four buttons. All four buttons turn yellow when the cursor is placed over them.

Next, you will modify your movie to show button tips with rollOvers.

1. Stop your movie.

2. Open the Cast window.

3. Select **cast member 9**, the play label. Place the label on the stage by the top button.

4. Select **cast member 10**, the stop label. Place the label on the stage by the second button.

5. Select **cast member 11**, the rewind label. Place the label on the stage by the third button.

6. Select **cast member 12**, the fast forward label. Place the label on the stage by the bottom button (see Figure 6.5).

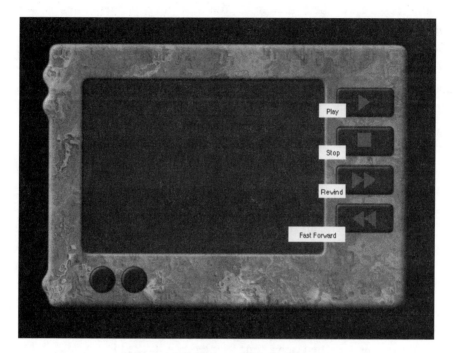

Figure 6.5 The stage with button tips.

Make sure cast members are in frames 1 and 2.

If the cursor is not on any of the buttons, then you don't want any of the button tips to show. If the cursor is on one of the buttons, only that button tip should be on the screen. Even though you have put the button tips on the stage for both frames 1 and 2, you can use Lingo to show the tips when you have a rollOver. You will use the Lingo property the visible of sprite. If the visible of sprite is TRUE, then the sprite is visible on the stage; if it is FALSE, then the sprite cannot be seen.

Open the frame script in frame 2. You will set up the first rollOver. You can use much of the script that is already there. Change the first two lines to read:

```
if rollOver (2) then set the visible of sprite 10 to TRUE
else set the visible of sprite 10 to FALSE
```

Comment the rest of the if-then lines. You can comment these lines using the **Comment** button in the Script window, **Shift-command-.** (period) on the Macintosh, or **Shift-Ctrl-.** on Windows.

Close the Script window and then rewind and play your movie. Notice you don't see the Button tip for the **Play** button. The cursor is not on the button, so the visible of sprite 10 is FALSE. Place the cursor over the first button. The Button tool tip is visible. Remove the cursor from the button. The Button tool tip goes away. Stop your movie.

When the visible of sprite = FALSE, it is equivalent to turning off the channel using the **Diamond** shaped button to the left of the channel number in the score.

Open the score and arrange it so that you can see channel 10 and the buttons at the same time. Play your movie, keeping the score open. Notice that the **Diamond** button in the score at channel 10 is depressed, turning off that channel (see Figure 6.7).

Place the cursor on the top button. The **Diamond** button in the score pops back up, turning the channel back on (see Figure 6.8).

Stop your movie, then open your frame script located in frame 2. Try setting up the rest of the rollOvers yourself. If you have problems, refer to the following script:

```
on exitFrame
      if rollOver (2) then set the visible of sprite 10 to TRUE
        else set the visible of sprite 10 to FALSE
      if rollOver (3) then set the visible of sprite 11 to TRUE
      else set the visible of sprite 11 to FALSE
      if rollOver (4) then set the visible of sprite 12 to TRUE
```

```
  else set the visible of sprite 12 to FALSE
  if rollOver (5) then set the visible of sprite 13 to TRUE
  else set the visible of sprite 13 to FALSE
   go to the frame
end
```

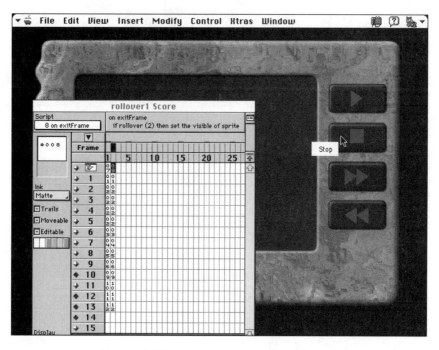

Figure 6.7 Using Lingo to turn off the channel.

On slower processors, it is possible that the tool tips in frame 1 will show for a split second while the movie makes its way to frame 2. To stop this from happening, you will set the visible of the tool tip sprites to **FALSE** in a startMovie handler. You can use a repeat loop similar to the one you used to puppet the sprites to set the states of the sprites.

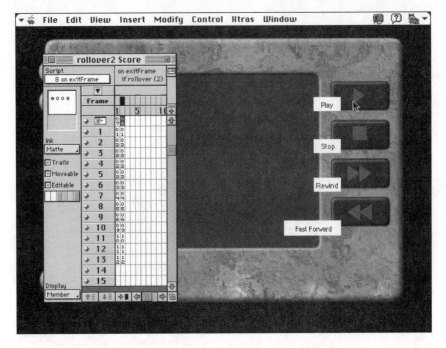

Figure 6.8 Using Lingo to turn the channel back on.

Open your movie script. At the top of the Script window, add the following handler:

```
on startMovie
     repeat with x=10 to 13
          set the visible of sprite x to FALSE
     end repeat
end
```

The startMovie script will make the sprites in channels 10 through 13 (the button tool tips) invisible before the playback head enters frame 1. That way, they will not show up until a rollOver occurs.

Close the movie script and then rewind and play the movie. Try out your rollOvers.

Summary

There you have it: an exciting new way to add interactivity to your movie. In this chapter, you learned how to create rollOvers on buttons to indicate to the user the interactive feature of your presentation. You also used rollOvers to create pop-up Help features in your presentation. Along the way, you used the Message window to discover the numeric values of ink effects and how to make a sprite visible or invisible on the stage. Experiment with rollOvers on your own. Set them on your stage to navigate your user to different parts of your presentation. Use rollOvers in conjunction with QuickTime movies to start a movie playing. Incorporate rollOvers in a children's game that teaches them a foreign language. The possibilities are endless.

CHAPTER 7

CONTROLLING
DIGITAL VIDEO

Lingo used in this chapter:

```
movieRate
movieTime
rollOver
the clickOn
the ink of sprite
the foreColor of sprite
```

Have you ever noticed that when you have a digital video (in this case, a QuickTime movie) in your Director movie, when the playback head reaches it in the score, the digital video just starts playing immediately? In many cases, it would be more convenient if the digital movie started when you clicked on a button. Even better would be to give your user total control of the digital video, letting them also rewind, fast forward, or stop your video. Then the end users could navigate anywhere they want within the digital video. With Lingo, this is easy to do. You just need to use the Lingo term *the movieRate*. In this chapter, you will use the movieRate to script buttons that follow human interface guidelines to control a QuickTime video.

This book uses Macromedia's definition of digital video, which means digital video is either a video of QuickTime format on the Macintosh or QuickTime or Video for Windows on a PC.

N O T E

Introducing MovieRate

Controlling a movie's speed and direction is done with the sprite property called the *movieRate*. A movieRate of 1 will show your digital video playing forward at normal speed. A movieRate of 0 has the video stopped. A movieRate of -1 will play your video in reverse. You can also play the movie at rates greater than 1. However, your system may not be able to show all the frames in the video at a higher rate of speed, consequently dropping frames. Faster processors will drop fewer frames than slower processors.

If you try using the **movieRate** command with a sprite that is not a digital video, you will get the error "not a digital movie sprite."

N O T E

Getting Started

Open movie **Ch7com.dir** on the CD that accompanies this book. You may recognize this movie. It was the completed movie for Chapter 6 as well. Play the Director movie. Notice that you can see the first frame of the digital video, but the video itself is not playing. When you place the cursor on top of one of the buttons on the right-hand side of the stage, the button turns color, indicating that the button is active. Click on the top button. The video starts to play forward. While the video is playing, click the bottom button. The video plays faster. The audio is also sped up. Click back on the **Play** button. The video plays forward at normal speed again. Click on the second button from the bottom of the stage. The video plays backwards. Click the **Stop** button. The video stops on whatever frame it is on at that moment.

In this chapter, you will program the **Play**, **Stop**, **Rewind**, and **Fast Forward** buttons. You will learn how to program them as you see them here, as well as program the **Fast Forward** and **Rewind** buttons to perform their tasks only when the user holds down the button.

Pausing a Movie before Playing

Open the movie **Ch7.dir**. Look at the score. Notice the movie is only two frames long. A frame script of "go to the frame" is in frame 2 of the script channel. Also, you can tell from the score (see Figure 7.1) that all the active buttons you saw in the final movie use the same graphic.

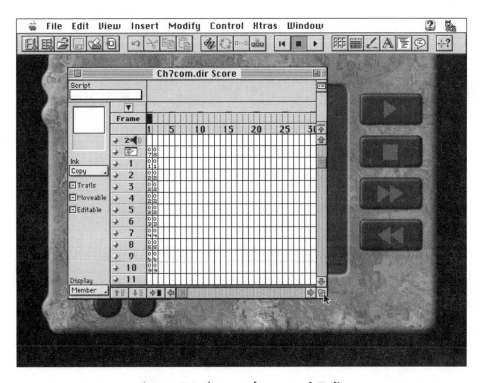

Figure 7.1 The score for movie **ch7.dir**.

Play the movie. The digital video starts to play. You don't want the video to play until you choose to play it by clicking the **Play** button. Your first task is to keep the video stopped until you want it to play. You can do this in the movie script.

Open the movie script and type the following handler:

```
on startMovie
    set the movieRate of sprite 10 to 0
end
```

Remember that a movieRate of 0 stops the video. You are setting the movieRate of sprite 10 because the QuickTime video is located in channel 10. Close the Movie Script window and rewind and play the movie. Now the QuickTime video doesn't start playing automatically. Your first task is done. Next you will script the buttons that will allow you to control the video. Because the four buttons perform four different tasks but are constructed out of the same graphic, you will need to use sprite scripts instead of cast scripts to do this.

Controlling Digital Video with the Play Button

Choose **frame 2, channel 2** and open a Script window. Create the following sprite script:

```
on mouseUp
    set the movieRate of sprite 10 to 1
end
```

A movieRate of 1 will play the digital video forward at normal speed.

Close the Script window and rewind and play your movie. Then click the **Play** button. The video starts to play. Now stop your movie.

Integrating Human Interface Guidelines

It would be nice if the **Play** button followed the human interface guidelines discussed earlier in this book. That would mean that when the user clicks the button, it changes in some way to indicate to the user that the button is selected. In this case, you will change the color of the play symbol and return it back to red after the user has clicked the **Play** button. You will change the color by using the property *the foreColor of sprite*, which is the foreground color of the cast member. This property only applies to 1-bit bitmap or shape cast members. Refer to Chapter 4 to learn how to color 1-bit cast members.

Right now the play symbol is red and the button is yellow. Green would be a good color to change it to. Pick a shade of green you like and find its corresponding color in the Color palette (see Figure 7.2). Color number 229 on the Mac system palette or 224 on the Windows system palette will work nicely.

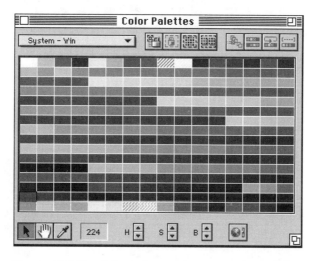

Figure 7.2 The Color palette and corresponding number.

Capturing Values in a Global Variable

There is one last thing to consider: You are about to change the foreground color of a sprite, then have it change back again. To make sure the button returns to its original color, capture the number of the color originally used so you can use it later. To capture this color and use it later, you will capture it in a global variable. You want a global variable because you are going to capture the color in a mouseDown handler and apply it in a mouseUp handler. In order for you to use a value in more than one handler, you need to use a global variable. Remember, when using a global variable, you must declare the variable in the Script window in which it is used.

Open your sprite script located at frame 2, channel 2. Change the Script window to read as shown in Figure 7.3.

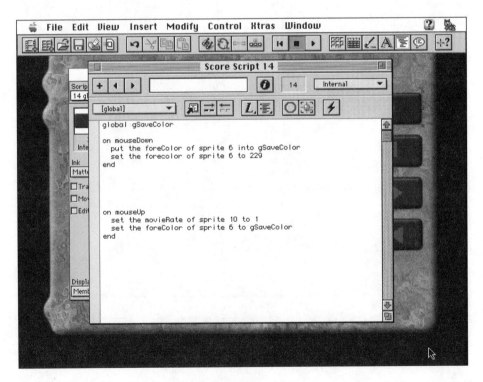

Figure 7.3 Your sprite script.

Close the Script window.

Puppeting More Sprites the Easy Way

In order for the sprite to change colors with the preceding Lingo, the sprite must be puppeted. The sprites that make up the buttons were already puppeted for you. Look at the frame script located in frame 1 of the script channel. You can edit the script so that it will puppet the sprites located on the buttons. Open the frame script located in frame 1 of the script channel.

```
on exitFrame
    repeat with x=2 to 5
        puppetsprite x, TRUE
    end repeat
end
```

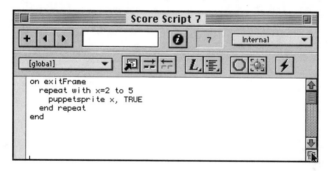

Figure 7.4

Right now, this script is puppeting the sprites in channels 2 through 5. Sprites in channels 6 through 9 need to be puppeted also. All you need to do is change one number in the preceding script and it will puppet channels 2 through 9.

Change the number 5 in the first line of the script to a 9:

```
on exitFrame
    repeat with x=2 to 9
        puppetSprite x, TRUE
    end repeat
end
```

Now all the channels from channel 2 through 9 are puppeted when the play-back head leaves frame 1 on its way to frame 2.

Close the Script window and rewind and play your movie. Then click the **Play** button.

The movie starts playing, but what about the color change? Director is changing the color but it's not showing you the change. You must tell Director to redraw the stage using the **updateStage** command.

Open the sprite script located at frame 2, channel 2. Add the **updateStage** command before the end statement in the *mouseDown* handler (see Figure 7.5).

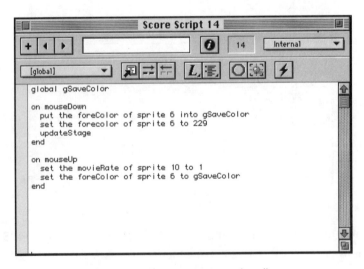

Figure 7.5 Your *mouseDown* handler.

Close the Script window and rewind and play your movie. Then click the **Play** button. The play symbol changes color, and the video starts playing. Notice that the play symbol remains green. You want it to turn back to red after it is clicked. You need to tell it to go back to its original color using Lingo and the *mouseUp* handler.

Now stop your movie and open the sprite script located at frame 2, channel 2. Add the following code to the *mouseUp* handler:

```
on mouseUp
     set the movieRate of sprite 10 to 1
     set the foreColor of sprite 6 to gsaveColor
end
```

Close the Sprite window. Rewind and play your movie and try out your new button. It works! You will script the **Stop** button now.

Creating a Stop Button

Open your sprite script located at frame 2, channel 2. Select the entire contents of the window and copy it. Open a sprite script located at frame 2, channel 3 and paste your sprite script in the window. Then change the movieRate from 1 to 0. Also, replace all instances of sprite 6 with sprite 7. Now close the window and save your movie. Play your movie, trying out both the **Play** and **Stop** buttons.

This script works as well. You could save yourself a lot of scripting if you placed the main *mouseDown* and *mouseUp* handlers in the movie script and then passed the items that are changing in them as arguments. Stop your movie and open the movie script. You need to create two user-defined handlers in here.

Creating User-Defined Handlers in the Movie Script

Paste your two handlers. They should still be on the clipboard of your computer. If they are not, open one of your sprite scripts, select the entire contents of the window, and copy it. Change the names of the handlers. Remember that most handlers in the movie script need to have user-defined names. If you like, you can use the handler names *up* and *down* again.

Creating Arguments

You also need to replace anything that will change from button to button. This includes sprite numbers and movieRates. You will replace these with arguments. Remember, an argument is a user-defined variable that recieves its value from elsewhere in the movie. For the sprite number, use the variable whichSprite. For movieRate, use whatSpeed.

Replace all sprite numbers that refer to a button with the argument whichSprite. In your *mouseUp* handler, you refer to sprite 10 in conjunction with the movieRate. This particular instance of a sprite number is not going to change because the movie is always going to be in channel 10. Leave this sprite number as is.

Replace the movieRate value with whatSpeed.

```
global gsaveColor

on down
    put the foreColor of sprite whichSprite into gsaveColor
    set the foreColor of sprite whichSprite  to 229
    updateStage
end

on up
    set the movieRate of sprite 10 to whatSpeed
    set the foreColor of sprite whichSprite to gsaveColor
end
```

Next, you need to tell Director that the variables you have placed in the movie score are arguments and will be receiving their values from some other script. To declare your arguments, add the argument names to the top line of the handler, immediately following the handler name (see Figure 7.6). Separate arguments with commas.

Now you need to call your handlers. Open the sprite script located at frame 2, channel 2.

Call your *down* and *up* movie handlers in your mouseDown and mouseUp handlers. You also need to place the values of the arguments in the same line that calls the handler:

```
on mouseDown
     down 6
end

on mouseUp
     up 6, 1
end
```

Remember, the first argument is the sprite number of the play symbol. The second argument is the movieRate of the QuickTime movie.

The sprite scripts no longer use the global variable gsaveColor, so you can delete the global declaration line located at the top of this sprite window.

Close the Script window and rewind and play your movie. Then try out the **Play** button. It should work just as it did when the entire script was in the sprite script. Stop your movie.

Copy the sprite script located on the **Play** button and paste it in the Script window for the **Stop** button. The sprite script for the **Stop** button is located at frame 2, channel 3. Change the whatSpeed argument to 0 and the whichSprite argument to 7:

```
on mouseDown
     down 7
end

on mouseUp
     up 7, 0
end
```

Now close the Sprite window.

You still need to script the **Fast Forward** and **Rewind** buttons, which is easy to do. You will use the same script you used for the first two buttons and simply change the arguments.

Scripting the Remaining Buttons

Open a sprite script for the **Fast Forward** button. Paste in your mouseUp and mouseDown scripts. Change the whatSpeed argument to a positive number greater than 1 and the whichSprite argument to 8. To minimize the number of frames dropped, use a value of 2 for whatSpeed.

```
on mouseDown
    down 8
end

on mouseUp
    up 8, 2
end
```

Close the sprite window and open a sprite script for the **Rewind** button. Paste in your mouseUp and mouseDown scripts. Then change the whatSpeed argument to a negative number and the whichSprite argument to 9. A value of -1 for whatSpeed will rewind the movie at the same absolute rate as a movieRate of 1. If you want to rewind the movie a little faster than that, use a value of -2.

```
on mouseDown
    down 9
end

on mouseUp
    up 9, -2
end
```

Close the Script window and rewind and play the movie. Then click all four buttons.

If the buttons aren't acting right, stop the movie and make sure you rewind it. If you don't rewind the movie before playing it, the frame script in the script channel of frame 1 will not be executed and your puppetSprites will not be turned on.

T I P

What happens if the user clicks on a button but then drags off of it? The symbol on the button should return to red. That is not happening. You need to test where the cursor is all the time the user is holding down the mouse button. To accomplish this, you will use a repeat loop and the Lingo term *rollOver* like in Chapter 5.

Open your movie script. You need to decide what is and isn't going to be in your repeat loop. You do not want the line *put the foreColor of sprite whichSprite into gsaveColor* in the repeat loop or it will keep trying to place a color into the variable gsaveColor, which means it will replace the original color with 229, completely negating why we created the variable in the first place. You do want to keep the foreColor green as long as the mouse button is held down and the cursor is on the button. If the mouse button is held down but moved off of the button, the foreColor of the button symbol, whether it is the play, stop, fast forward or reverse symbol to return to its original red color. So you want to make sure the rollOver test is in the repeat loop. You know from Chapter 5 that when you use the term *rollOver*, you need to also tell Director what sprite you are checking the rollOver for. So, if you were scripting the **Play** button, you would need to say:

```
if rollOver 2 then
     set the foreColor of sprite whichSprite to 229
else
     set the foreColor of sprite whichSprite to gsaveColor
end if
```

However, you are not always going to be selecting the **Play** button. You will be selecting any one of four buttons. The rollOver statement needs to be more generic; it cannot have a single numeric value. You could use another argument, or you could use a function that will place the appropriate sprite number in your script. The function you will use is *the clickOn*.

Remember, functions return values like *the frame* returns the current frame the playback head is in. *The clickOn* function returns the value of the last active sprite that was clicked on by the user. An active sprite has a sprite script attached to it. You can use *the clickOn* in all your handlers for the four buttons and not worry about what channel the buttons are in. *The clickOn* will capture that value for you.

Modify your *up* and *down* handlers, adding the lines in bold:

```
on down whichSprite
      put the foreColor of sprite whichSprite into gsaveColor
      repeat while the mouseDown
            if rollOver (the clickOn) then
                  set the foreColor of sprite whichSprite to 229
            else
                  set the foreColor of sprite whichSprite to gsaveColor
            end if
            updateStage
      end repeat
end

on up whichSprite, whatSpeed
      if rollOver (the clickOn) then
            set the movieRate of sprite 10 to whatSpeed
            set the foreColor of sprite whichSprite to gsaveColor
      else
            exit
      end if
end
```

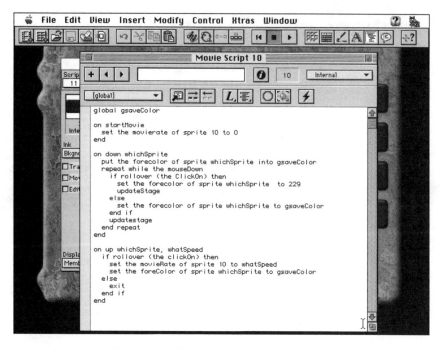

Figure 7.6 The movie handler for **ch7.dir**.

Close the movie script. Rewind and play your movie, trying out your buttons.

They all work! Now you can make some simple changes to make the buttons react exactly as you want them to. You will change the buttons to act two different ways. One is for the **Rewind** and **Fast Forward** buttons only to be active when the button is being held down. The other is for the **Rewind** button to automatically set the movie back to the beginning and the **Fast Forward** button to automatically to go to the last frame of the movie. You will first tackle the task of making the **Rewind** and **Fast Forward** buttons work only when they are being held down. To see this alteration in action, open the movie **ch7com2.dir**. Play the movie. Click and hold down on the **Rewind** button. The movie rewinds. Let go of the mouse button. The movie stops rewinding. Try the **Fast Forward** button. It works the same way. The modifications you need to make to have the **Fast Forward** and **Rewind** buttons operate this way are very similar to what you just did for the rollOvers.

Variations on a Theme

Open the movie script and look at your two customized handlers.

You want the movie to rewind while the mouse is held down but your command for movieRate is located in the handler that reacts to the mouseUp event. You will not be able to use the scripts here. You will use the same lines of code, but in different locations.

Open the sprite script for the **Rewind** button. It is located at frame 2, channel 5. Change your mouseDown script to read:

```
on mouseDown
    put the foreColor of sprite 9 into gsaveColor
    repeat while the mouseDown
        if rollOver (the clickOn) then
            set the foreColor of sprite 9  to 229
            set the movieRate of sprite 10 to -2
        end if
        updateStage
    end repeat
end
```

Again, you need to make sure the code that captures the original color is *not* in the repeat loop. Although it will capture the correct color once, it would then capture the foreColor as 229, which would not allow you to reset the color back to its original pigment. Also, now that you are using the gsaveColor global variable in this handler again, you need to declare the global variable as the first line in the Script window.

If you tried your buttons now, you would find that the digital video will rewind when the button is held down, but will continue to rewind once the button is let go. Not only that, but if the user clicks the **Rewind** button then drags off of it, the button does not return to its original color like you want it to. You need to add a few lines to your *mouseDown* handler.

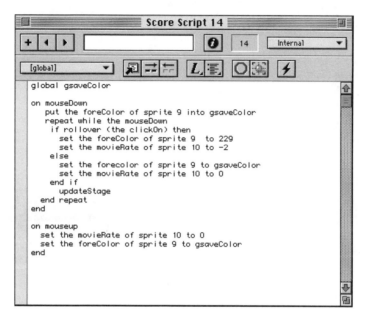

Figure 7.7 Your mouseDown script.

Add the following *else* statement to your handler:

```
else
   set the foreColor of sprite 9 to gsaveColor
   set the movieRate of sprite 10 to 0
```

Close the Script window and rewind and play your movie (Figure 7.7). Then try your **Rewind** button.

As long as the mouse is held down, it works properly. If you let go of the mouse button while not on the button it works, but what about if you just simply click the **Rewind** button? The color is not restored, and the movie is still rewinding. You need to alter the *mouseUp* handler so the movie stops rewinding and the red color is restored to the rewind symbol after you click the **Rewind** button.

Change the *mouseUp* handler to read as follows:

```
on mouseUp
    set the movieRate of sprite 10 to 0
    set the foreColor of sprite 9 to gsaveColor
end
```

Close the Script window. Rewind and play your movie, trying out the **Rewind** button.

Now the movie rewinds only for as long as the button is held down. Why is there no if-then-else structure here? Because in this case, you don't care if the user is on the button or not. In both instances, you want the same thing to happen: for the movie to stop and the original color to be restored.

Now you can create the same type of functionality for the **Fast Forward** button.

Stop your movie and open the sprite script for the **Rewind** button. Select all the text in the Script window and copy it. Open the sprite script attached to the **Fast Forward** button. It is located at frame 2, channel 4. Select the contents of the window and choose **Paste** from the Edit menu.

The *mouseDown* and *mouseUp* handlers from the **Rewind** button are now in place. Change any instances of sprite 9 to sprite 8. This will make sure that the **Fast Forward** symbol located in channel 8 of the score turns green.

Also change the movieRate from -2 to +2 in the *mouseDown* handler. Close the Script window. Rewind and play your movie, trying out the **Fast Forward** button. It should only fast forward while the button is held down.

Using MovieTime

Last, you will make the **Rewind** button automatically rewind the movie to the first frame, and the **Fast Forward** button will bring the movie to its last frame. Open and play the movie **Ch7com3.dir**. Click on the **Play** button. Let the video play for a few seconds. Now click the **Rewind** button. The movie goes back to the first frame and plays from there. Click the **Fast Forward** button. You are now on the last frame of the movie and the movie stops.

To make the **Rewind** and **Fast Forward** buttons work like this, you need to use the property *the MovieTime*. Again this property is for digital video sprites. You measure the length of the movie using *MovieTime*, which is measured in ticks with 60 ticks in a second. The length of the movie measured in *movieTime* is a constant. The digital video will always contain the same amount of ticks whether you are using a Mac Plus or a Pentium. The length of digital video is not dependent on the processor speed. The first frame of the movie has a movieTime of 0. You need to find out the movieTime for the end of the movie, or find out how many ticks are in the movie.

Play your Director movie and click the **Play** button. Let the entire video play. Open the Message window and type **put the movieTime of sprite 10** and press the **Return** key. The Message window returns the value 960 (see Figure 7.8).

Figure 7.8 Using the Message window to find the length of a QuickTime movie.

Now you can script the **Rewind** and **Fast Forward** buttons. Open the sprite script for the **Fast Forward** button. It is located at frame 2, channel 4.

Delete the repeat loop and the if-then-else statement. Change the handler to use movieTime instead of movieRate and to incorporate the movieTime you just found in the Message window. Your handler should look like this:

```
on mouseDown
     put the foreColor of sprite 8 into gsaveColor
     set the foreColor of sprite 8  to 229
     set the movieTime of sprite 10 to 960
     updateStage
end
```

Your *mouseUp* handler should stay the same.

Close your Script window and rewind and play your movie. Click the **Play** button. Again, let the video play for a few seconds.

Now click the **Fast Forward** button. The video goes to its last frame then stops. You need to make similar changes to your **Rewind** button. Stop your movie.

Open sprite script for the **Rewind** button. It is located at frame 2, channel 5. Alter the *mouseDown* script to look like the following:

```
on mouseDown
     put the foreColor of sprite 9 into gsaveColor
     set the foreColor of sprite 9  to 229
     set the movieTime of sprite 10 to 0
     updateStage
end
```

You also need to make one change to your *mouseUp* handler. This time, after the movie rewinds, you want it to start playing forward again.

In your *mouseUp* handler, change the movieRate to 1.

```
on mouseUp
     set the movieRate of sprite 10 to 1
     set the foreColor of sprite 9 to gsaveColor
end
```

Close the Script window and rewind and play your movie. Then click the **Play** button. Let the QuickTime play for a few seconds. Click the **Rewind** button. The video rewinds to the first frame and starts over again. Next click the **Fast Forward** button. The video goes to the last frame of the QuickTime. Now you are a pro at controlling digital video playback!

Summary

In this chapter, you controlled the digital video and learned how to make it remain paused until the user clicks a button. Using movieTime, you can play the video forward or backward at different speeds. You also learned how to keep the movieTime constant while a button is held down and how to stop it when the button is let go. You are getting some great experience with button handlers! The more you do them the easier they get.

Any digital video you use will play at a constant rate, no matter what type of computer you are play it on. That is, a digital video will take the same amount of time to play on a Mac Plus or a 100MHz Pentium. Director will tell you how long the movie is in ticks (a *tick* is 1/60 of a second). You can then use that measurement in conjunction with *the movieTime* to control your digital video. In the next chapter, you will use *the movieTime* to synchronize the video with stage events.

CHAPTER 8

SYNCHRONIZATION OF VIDEO AND SCREEN EVENTS

Lingo included in this chapter:

```
MovieRate
MovieTime
```

Wouldn't it be great to be able to synchronize stage events with narration, music, or digital video so that regardless of the computer you used to play back your movie, the stage events and sound will stay in synch? Now you can, with Lingo. This chapter shows you how.

A sample of digital video will play for the same amount of time regardless of the computer you play it on. The processor type and speed do not affect the length of the digital video. In Director, you measure the time of a digital video in ticks. One tick is 1/60 of a second.

Getting Started

Open the movie **ch8com.dir** on the CD accompanying this book. Play the movie. You see the text of the QuickTime video along the bottom of the stage. Stop the movie. Look at the score (Figure 8.1).

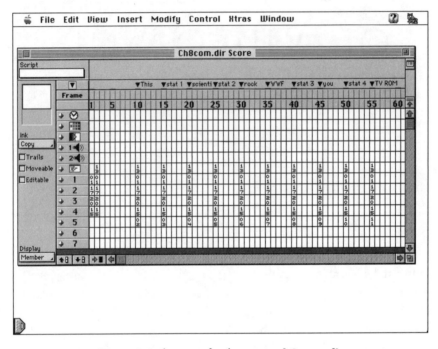

Figure 8.1 The score for the movie **ch8com.dir**.

You see several single frames, each marked with a label. Each one of those frames contains part of the text you saw. At every frame where there is text, there is also the frame script, "go to the frame," which keeps the playback head in place until the next movieTime is detected. Your mission, should you choose to accept it, is to find the movieTimes for certain events and direct the playback head to the corresponding frame when the movieTime matches certain numbers.

Finding MovieTimes

1. Open the movie **ch8.com**.
2. Play the movie. You see the video play. You will add the "close captioning" to the video.
3. Stop the movie.

Notice that there is already a frame script in many of the frames. That script is simply, *go to the frame*.

First you will need to find the movieTimes for each piece of narration from the movie as well as when the static starts. So that you know what the text is, the script is printed here:

```
...this Thursday evening.   Thanks for joining us.
<static>
- scientists...
- things that are mad
<static>
- Rock's back...
- yeah!   Rock!
- in the WWF
<static>
- ...you risk nothing.   Have your credit card handy...
<static>
<chimes>
```

Now, how do you find out the movieTime of each event? You will create a field on the screen that will display the movieTime as the movie plays.

Choose **Tools** form the Window menu, and then choose the **Field** tool from the palette. Click on the top of the screen; a field box appears on the stage. Type **123** in the field (see Figure 8.2).

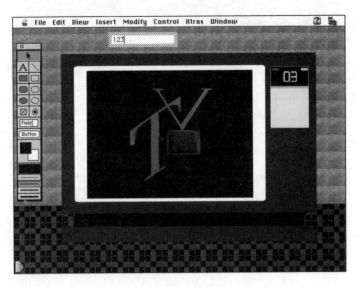

Figure 8.2 Creating a field castmember.

Select the **Cast** window and choose the field member in the Cast window. Then name the field "movie text," as shown in Figure 8.3.

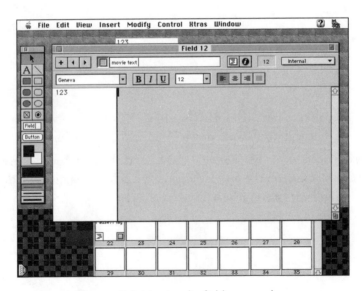

Figure 8.3 Naming the field castmember.

Next you will tell Director to put the movieTime values in this field member. Open the frame script located in frame 1. Add the following line to the frame script:

```
put the movieTime of sprite 1 into "movie time"
```

Close the Script window and play the movie.

You will see the movieTime flying by. Remember, movieTime is measured in ticks, with 60 ticks per second. You need to find the individual movieTime for certain events. The events you need to time are when each piece of narration starts and when the static starts.

Next, you will create a way to control the movie so that you can start it and stop it at will and take note of the movieTime. You will create a button to control the movie. Select the **Button** tool from the Tools palette. Click on the stage. Type **Play/Pause** on the button.

You will now script the button to toggle between playing the video and stopping it. You can use a cast script to do this.

Select the button in the Cast window and click the **Script** button. Type the following script in the Script window:

```
on mouseUp
    if the movieRate of sprite 1 = 1 then
        set the movieRate  of sprite 1 to 0
    else
        set the movieRate of sprite 1 to 1
    end if
end
```

If the video is playing, you want to use the button to stop it to find the movieTime of that particular frame of the video. If it's not playing, and you've already marked down the movieTime, you want to use the button to start the video playing where it left off. The previous script notes whether the video is playing or not by checking the movieRate of the video. Remember from the last chapter, if the video is playing, its movieRate equals 1. If it is not playing, the movieRate equals 0. Close the Script window. You are ready to mark down the movie times. Now rewind and play the movie.

Refer to the previous script and mark down the movieTimes when narration begins and the static begins. Use your **Play/Pause** button to help you find the movieTimes. Don't worry about getting the exact movieTimes, you can always edit them later.

Following is a set of numbers that will be used for this chapter. Your numbers may be a bit different. You can use either your own movieTime numbers or these:

MovieTime

45	...this Thursday evening. Thanks for joining us.
130	<static>
155	- scientists...
	- things that are mad
360	<static>
400	- Rock's back...
	- yeah! Rock!
550	- in the WWF
600	<static>
620	- ...you risk nothing. Have your credit card handy...
750	<static>
770	<chimes>

It's time to use the movieTimes in conjunction with the close captions. You need your movie to constantly check what the movieTime of the video is. Previously, when you needed an action to be repeated, you used a repeat loop such as "repeat while the mouseDown." This loop will not work here because there is no keypress or mouseclick happening. There is a place where you can tell Director to check the movieTime. That is in the frame script. The frame script *go to the frame* keeps the playback head in motion. So you can tell Director to keep checking the movieTime in that script. Just put the code that actually checks the movieTime in the move script and call that handler from the frame script. This is the user defined handler named *checkIt*.

Once you have the movieTimes, you no longer need the field castmember on the stage. Delete the field castmember from the score and open the frame script located in channel 2. Remove the following line from the handler:

```
put the movieTime of sprite 1 into field "movie time"
```

You no longer need the movieTime running at the top of the stage. Place the handler name *checkIt* in the frame script (see Figure 8.4).

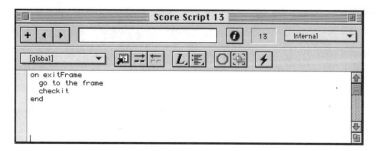

Figure 8.4 The revised frame script.

All the other frame scripts are instances of the same script, so you do not need to add the handler name in all the other frame scripts; the name is already there. Now close the frame script and open your movie script. You need to create the following *checkIt* handler:

```
on checkIt
    if the movieTime of sprite 1 > 45 then go to "this"
end
```

If you used the code:

```
if the movieTime of sprite 1 = 45 then go to "this"
```

The code would not be executed unless the playback head checks this handler when the movieTime is exactly 45. You cannot assume this is going to happen. The playback head has so many things to do, and the movieTime is measured in such small increments, chances are that it won't check the movieTime at that exact tick. The word *this* is a label already located in the score. It is the position where the words for the first piece of narration are placed on the stage.

Add the following line of code to the handler before trying it out:

```
if the movieTime of sprite 1 > 130 then go to "stat 1"
```

Close the movie script. Rewind your movie and play it. The first piece of narration appears on the stage at the right time, but when you get to the second piece, the two pieces fight each other for placement on the stage. Now stop your movie.

The movie time has gone beyond 130. Now every time the playback head reads the *checkIt* handler, it tries to execute both lines of code. We have a lower bound for the movieTime, but we need an upper bound so that the playback head has only one possible position.

Open your movie script. Modify the handler by adding the following bold code:

```
if the movieTime of sprite 1 > 45 and the movieTime of ¬
sprite 1 < 55 then go to "this"
if the movieTime of sprite 1 > 130 and the movieTime of ¬
sprite 1 < 140 then go to "stat 1"
```

The upper bounds are chosen by adding 10 ticks to the lower bound. You can have more or fewer ticks but with more ticks, the playback head sometimes branches later than you want. If you have fewer ticks, there is a possibility of missing the branching altogether. Also, the upper bound may need to be altered depending on the Director movie tempo. If the tempo is slow, it will slow down how often the handler *checkIt* is called. Do not be afraid to experiment with the upper bound.

Even though the digital movie is the same length regardless of the computer it is played on, you should always test your presentation on as many systems as you can to make sure the playback will be smooth on all platforms.

N O T E

Close the movie script and rewind and play your movie. The close captions for the beginning of the movie work!

Now that you see how the movieTime works, you can construct the rest of the movie script. To help you out, here are the remaining labels in the score listed in the order that they appear:

```
scientists
stat 2
rock
WWF
stat 3
you
stat 4
TV ROM
```

Now you have a QuickTime movie completely in synch with screen events. You can use this same technique with graphics or even sound files to make spectacular presentations or marketing material and not have to worry about what type of computer it will be played back on. It will remain in synch on a Pentium-based windows machine or a Macintosh SI.

NOTE The movie will remain in synch no matter what platform is used for playback because on slower machines, a certain number of visual frames will be dropped in order for the audio and video to stay in synch.

If you are having problems getting things in synch, refer to the following completed movie script:

```
on checkit
 if the movietime of sprite 1> 45 and the movietime of sprite 1<55
then go to "this"
  if the movietime of sprite 1> 130 and the movietime of sprite
1<140 then go to "stat 1"
  if the movietime of sprite 1> 155 and the movietime of sprite
1<165 then go to "scientists"
  if the movietime of sprite 1 > 360 and the movietime of sprite
```

```
1<370 then go to "stat 2"
  if the movietime of sprite 1 > 400 and the movietime of sprite 1
<410 then go to "rock"
  if the movietime of sprite 1 > 550 and the movietime of sprite
1<560 then go to "WWF"
  if the movietime of sprite 1 > 600 and the movietime of sprite
1<610 then go to "stat 3"
  if the movietime of sprite 1 > 620 and the movietime of sprite
1<630 then go to "you"
  if the movietime of sprite 1 > 750 and the movietime of sprite
1<760 then go to "stat 4"
  if the movietime of sprite 1 > 770 and the movietime of sprite
1<780 then go to "TV ROM"
end
```

Summary

QuickTime and Video for Windows are created differently from other animation formats. In these video formats, the sound is linked to certain frames of the video, creating a synchronous playback between the audio and video. If the video is playing back and comes to a linked frame, it will drop other video frames in order to play the linked frames in synch. You can take advantage of this in Director by using the movieTime property. Once you find the specific movieTime of a frame of the video, you can match the screen events with the video.

CHAPTER 9

FUN WITH SPRITES

Lingo included in this chapter:

```
the locH of sprite
the locV of sprite
mouseH
mouseV
sprite x within sprite y
the clickOn
soundBusy
the movableSprite
```

This chapter shows techniques to allow your user to move sprites around the stage and receive feedback, depending on where they move them to. These techniques are used in kiosks, games, educational titles, just about anywhere! This is true interactivity. Instead of users clicking on a button, they physically manipulate events on the screen. In this chapter, you will build a simple language game where the user must match the correct Spanish word to its color.

Getting Started

Open the movie **ch9COM.dir** on the CD that accompanies this book. Play the movie. The idea here is to label the colored blocks with the correct word in Spanish. Drag the word *azul* onto the red block. Notice it moves back to its starting point. Drag *azul* again, this time to the blue block. The word stays on the block this time, and you hear the word spoken. Match the other words with their colors. Now open the score (see Figure 9.1).

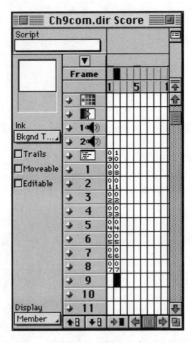

Figure 9.1 The score for the movie **Ch9Com.dir**.

Notice only two frames are being used. All the interactivity is achieved with Lingo.

Setting Up

By now, you should have a pretty good understanding of how Lingo works. You might not know all the commands you need, but you should have a sense as to what you need to do in Lingo. For you to be able to move the words around, changing their location compared to where they are located in the score, you will need to puppet them so they will obey your Lingo instead of what is in the score. Also, as you have only two frames in the score, but the movie is not ending right away, there must be a command to tell the movie to keep running in frame 2. You will set up these scripts first.

Open the movie **ch9.dir** on this book's CD ROM. You will puppet the appropriate sprites first. The sprites that need to be puppeted are the ones that are going to move according to Lingo instead of according to the score. Those sprites are the ones that are the Spanish words in channels 5 through 7.

Open a frame script in frame 1 and create the following handler:

```
on exitFrame
      repeat with x = 5 to 7
            puppetSprite x, TRUE
      end repeat
end
```

The sprites that need to respond to Lingo are located in channels 5, 6, and 7 of the score. Notice that you can use the above "shorthand" or loop to puppet sprites when the sprites you need to control with Lingo are in sequential channels of the score. Close the Script window. Next you need to tell the movie to keep playing in frame 2.

Pause versus Go to the Frame

There is also a Lingo command, **pause**, which is often used in a frame script. The difference between **pause** and **go to the frame** is that **pause** stops the playback head from moving. If the playback head is not moving, sound, film loops, and QuickTime movies will stop. Usually this is not what you want to happen, although sometimes it works to your advantage. If you have a frame where you want the playback head to wait for the user to click a button and it contains a transition, the playback head will continually play the frame AND the transition if you use go to the frame. If you use pause instead, the frame and the transition plays once, which, chances are , is what you want to happen. With **go to the frame**, the entire frame is repeated including the transition. Now you have two ways to keep the playback head in a frame, you can choose which one is better for your situation.

Open a frame script in frame 2 and create the following handler:

```
on exitFrame
     go to the frame
end
```

Close the Script window.

Now play the movie and try moving the words. They stay where they are because you need to tell the sprites to follow the movement of the mouse, which is done through Lingo. Stop the movie.

One property of every sprite is its location. The location of a sprite is defined by two components called locH and locV. LocH is the sprite's horizontal location on the stage measured in pixels. LocV is the vertical location of the sprite on the stage. So, if you have a stage set for a 13" monitor, its dimensions are 640 pixels by 480 pixels. The top-left corner of the stage has the coordinates 0 horizontal X 0 vertical. You can set the location of any sprite using *the locH of sprite* and *the locV of sprite*. There is also a Lingo property *the loc of sprite*, whose values are given as a point. A point consists of two numbers, the horizontal location and the vertical location. To locate the current location of a sprite on the stage, open the Message window and type:

```
put the loc of sprite 6
```

The Message window returns the point (see Figure 9.2):

Figure 9.2 The Message window returning the location of a sprite as a point.

In this chapter, you will use locH and locV to tell the sprite to follow the mouse around. You will place this Lingo in a sprite script.

Select the cell located in the score at frame 2, channel 5. You will place a sprite script on the word *azul*. Open a Script window and create the following handler:

```
on mouseDown
     set the locH of sprite 5 to mouseH
     set the locV of sprite 5 to mouseV
     updateStage
end
```

MouseH and mouseV are the horizontal and vertical placement of the cursor on the stage. Right now, as soon as the mouse is clicked, the word *azul* will center itself on the mouse location. You want it to continually change its location as long as the mouse is held down. You need to tell Director, as long as the mouse is held down, to keep setting the vertical and horizontal location of the sprite equal to the location of the cursor. You need to add a repeat loop. Modify your handler to look like the following:

```
on mouseDown
  repeat while the mouseDown
     set the locH of sprite 5 to mouseH
     set the locV of sprite 5 to mouseV
     updateStage
  end repeat
end
```

Close the Script window and rewind and play your movie. Try dragging the word *azul*. It now follows the cursor around the stage. Next, you want something to happen when the word is left somewhere. If the word is left on the correct color block, it will stay there. If it is on the wrong color block, you want it to return to its starting position. Instead of worrying about finding the exact coordinates for every sprite, you will use a global variable to store the coordinates. You will use goldLocH to store the original horizontal location and goldLocV to store the original vertical location. Now stop your movie.

Capturing the Location of the Sprite

Open your sprite script again. You need to declare your global variable at the top of the Script window. Type the following declaration line at the top of the window:

```
global gOldLocV, gOldLocH
```

After the on mouseDown code (see Figure 9.3), add:

```
set the locH of sprite 5 to gOldLocH
set the locV of sprite 5 to gOldLocV
```

```
on mouseDown
    put the locH of sprite 5 into gOldLocH
    put the locV of sprite 5 into gOldLocV
    repeat while the mouseDown
      set the Loch of sprite 5 to the mouseH
      set the locV of sprite 5 to the mouseV
      updatestage
    end repeat
end
```

Figure 9.3 The *mouseDown* handler.

Now it's time to create the *mouseUp* handler. One of two things will happen. Either the word will stay where the user has left it and a sound will play or it will return to its original position. You need Director to detect whether the word is in the right box. To do this, you will use the *sprite...within* comparison operator. If the word is within the correct box, then the word will stay there; if the word is not within the right box, then it moves back. For now, if the word is in the right place, you will hear a beep. You will modify it later to play a puppetSound.

Creating Response Based on User Placement of Sprite

Create the following *mouseUp* handler:

```
on mouseUp
    if sprite 5 within sprite 3 then
        beep
```

```
    else
            set the locH of sprite 5 to goldLocH
            set the locV of sprite 5 to goldLocV
            updateStage
    end if
end
```

Sprite 3 is the blue box. Because *azul* means blue, you want the word to be inside the box.

Close the script box and rewind and play the movie. Then drag the word *azul* onto the red box. It should go back to its original position. Now drag it to the blue box. The word stays there, and the computer beeps! You have one word done. Before scripting the other words, it would be best to create user-defined handlers out of the sprite script. Then the other words will be easier to program.

Creating User-Defined Handlers in the Movie Script

Open your sprite script and select the contents of the window and cut them. Open your movie script and choose **Paste** from the Edit menu.

Any instances where a different sprite is going to be called needs a variable instead of a sprite number. In this particular example, any instance to a sprite number will be turned into an argument. That means that it will receive its value from somewhere else. In this case, it will get the values it needs from the sprite script. These arguments are user-defined and cannot be Lingo terms. Let's use *whichWord* for the sprite that contains one of the Spanish words and *whichBlock* when you need to refer to which box the user has placed the word in.

Change all instances of sprite 5 to sprite whichWord. Change the instance to sprite 3 to whichBlock. Remember that sprite 3 refers to which color box matches the Spanish word. Your handlers should look like the following ones:

```
on mouseDown
     set the locH of sprite whichWord to goldLocH
     set the locV of sprite whichWord to gOldLocV
     repeat while the mouseDown
          set the locH of sprite whichWord to mouseH
          set the locV of sprite whichWord to mouseV
          updateStage
     end repeat
end

on mouseUp
     if sprite whichWord within sprite whichBlock then
          beep
     else
          set the locH of sprite whichWord to goldLocH
          set the locV of sprite whichWord to goldLocV
          updateStage
     end if
end
```

There are two more things you need to do to these handlers. They need user-defined names instead of *on mouseUp* and *on mouseDown*. Also, you need to tell Director what elements of your scripts are arguments. To do that, you place the arguments after the handler name. It is best to name handlers in such a way that you can tell their functionality by looking at the name. For here, let's call these two *up* and *down*.

Change the names of your handlers and add the arguments. Your finished movie script will look like Figure 9.4.

Now that you have created these new handlers, you need to call them, or in other words, tell Director when it should execute the code within the handlers. You want that code to be executed whenever someone drags around a word. You also need to pass values for the arguments you just placed in the handlers in the movie script. Close your movie script.

Figure 9.4 Your movie script with user-defined handlers and arguments.

Calling Handlers and Defining Arguments

Open a sprite script at frame 2, channel 5. This script will be for if they drag the word *azul*. Create the following *mouseUp* and *mouseDown* handlers:

```
on mouseDown
     down (the clickOn)
end
on mouseUp
     up (the clickOn), 3
end
```

You could have used the number that corresponds to the channel in which the word *azul* is located. However, the function *the clickOn* finds out the number for you. Either way will work. In the *mouseUp* handler, you need two arguments, one for the word being dragged and the other for what box the user is putting it into. So now, when the user begins to drag a word, it triggers the Down handler in the movie script. Director checks what channel that word is in and places that channel number in the Down handler any place it sees the term *whichWord*. When the user lets go of the word, the Up handler in the movie script is activated. Again, Director checks to see what channel the sprite that was just dragged is in and places that number wherever it sees the word *whichWord*. The number 3 is also passed to the Up handler and is placed wherever the word *whichBlock* is located.

Select the contents of the Script window and copy them. Close the Script window. Now you can script the other two words easily.

Open a sprite script for the sprite in channel 6, frame 2. Paste your two handlers into the Script window. You need to change the arguments so they will work with the word *verde* instead of *azul*. Change the number 3 in the *mouseUp* handler to a 4.

```
on mouseDown
      down (the clickOn)
end

on mouseUp
      up (the clickOn), 4
end
```

Notice because you're using the clickOn instead of a channel number, you don't even need to change that particular argument. Director makes the changes for you. You need to change only one thing, and that is the channel in which the corresponding color box for the particular Spanish word is located. In this case, the green box is in channel 4.

Close the Script window and open a sprite script for channel 7, frame 2. Paste your *mouseDown* and *mouseUp* handlers in the window. These two handlers should still be on the clipboard of your computer.

Change the 3 in the *mouseUp* handler into a 2. The word *rojo* belongs with the red box, which is located in channel 2. Now close the sprite Script window. Rewind and play your movie and then place *rojo* on the blue box. It goes back to its original position. Now place *rojo* on the red box. The computer beeps and the word stays there. Congratulations! You just created your first educational application using Lingo!

You can make some simple modifications to enhance the game. You will add the audio of the words when the user places the words correctly on the boxes, and you will change the *mouseUp* script so the user cannot move the word off of the color box once it is placed correctly.

Adding PuppetSounds

Open the movie script. You want the sound to play after the word is placed in the correct spot. That means you want it in the Up handler. You will use a puppetSound to play the sound. Because the sound is going to change depending on what word is placed, you will need to use an argument and then pass the correct sound via a sprite script.

Replace the word *beep* in the Up handler with:

```
puppetSound whichSound
```

Add the word *whichSound* to the list of arguments for the Up handler. Your movie script should look like:

```
on Down, whichWord
      set the locH of sprite whichWord to goldLocH
      set the locV of sprite whichWord to gOldLocV
      repeat while the mouseDown
          set the locH of sprite whichWord to mouseH
          set the locV of sprite whichWord to mouseV
          updateStage
      end repeat
end

on Up, whichWord, whichBlock, whichSound
```

```
    if sprite whichWord within sprite whichBlock then
        puppetSound whichsound
    else
        set the locH of sprite whichWord to goldLocH
        set the locV of sprite whichWord to goldLocV
        updateStage
    end if
end
```

Now you need to define which sound to play with every word. You will do that in your sprite scripts. Open the sprite script located in channel 5, frame 2. Add the value for the argument *whichSound*. In this case, it is the word *azul*. The *mouseUp* handler should look like:

```
on up
     up (the clickOn), 3, "azul"
end
```

NOTE   Make sure the word *azul* has quotes around it.

For the sprite script located in channel 6, frame 2, add the value **verde** to the list of arguments. Add the value **rojo** to the list of arguments located in the sprite script attached to the cell in channel 7, frame 2. Rewind and play your movie. Now place the words on the correct color boxes. You hear the word being spoken.

In this particular example, everything works fine but what if you had another sound playing in sound channel 1 when there were no puppetSounds? You have turned on the puppetSounds and never turned them off. This means that whatever may be in the sound channel 1 will never play once the first puppetSound command is executed. You need to issue the **puppetSound 0** command to return control to the score. The dilemma is that if you issue it too fast, you won't hear the entire word. It will get clipped off. You want to turn off the puppetSound after the word is done, not before. This can be done using the *soundBusy* function, which determines whether a sound is playing in the specified channel. If a sound is being played, **soundBusy** returns the value of 1 or TRUE. If no sound is being played, then the function returns the value of 0 or FALSE. So you can tell Director that no sound is playing, execute the command, **puppetSound 0**.

Turning off the PuppetSound

Open your movie script. In the Up handler, add the following bold lines:

```
on Down, whichWord
     set the locH of sprite whichWord to goldLocH
     set the locV of sprite whichWord to gOldLocV
     repeat while the mouseDown
          set the locH of sprite whichWord to mouseH
          set the locV of sprite whichWord to mouseV
          updateStage
     end repeat
end

on Up, whichWord, whichBlock, whichSound
     if sprite whichWord within sprite whichBlock then
          puppetSound whichsound
          repeat while soundBusy (1)
               nothing
          end repeat
          puppetSound 0
     else
          set the locH of sprite whichWord to goldLocH
          set the locV of sprite whichWord to goldLocV
          updateStage
     end if
end
```

The repeat loop makes the movie wait until the sound is finished. Then it will turn off the puppetSound and return control to the score.

Setting the *MovableSprite of Sprite* Property

The last thing you need to do is make sure the user cannot move the word off the color box once it is placed correctly. Again, this will take place in the Up handler. In the Down handler, you told Director to move the sprite wherever the cursor moves. Now you want to tell it not to move once the sprite is in the right place. You will use *the movableSprite of sprite* property. This property can be true or false. It is true if the sprite can move; it is FALSE if the sprite cannot move.

Add the following line before the repeat loop in the Up handler (see also Figure 9.5, the final movie script.):

```
set the movableSprite of sprite whichWord to FALSE
```

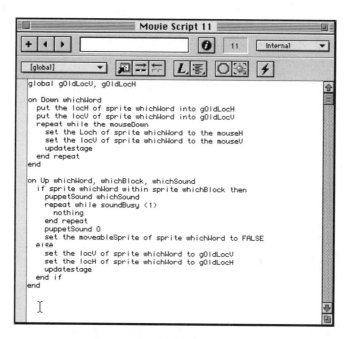

Figure 9.5 The final movie script.

Close the movie script. Rewind and play your movie. Then place the words on the right color boxes. Try placing the words somewhere else. The words appear as if they can still move, but when you let go of them, they pop back onto their color boxes.

Summary

Every sprite has a particular location on the stage. This location is made up of two coordinates, the horizontal location and the vertical location. These locations are measured in pixels. The location is measured from the registration point, usually located in the middle of the sprite for a bitmap and the upper-left corner for a quickDraw item (a shape created using the Tools palette). The registration of a bitmap can be changed in the Paint window using the Registration tool.

The location of the sprite can be changed in many ways. If you want to use Lingo to change the location, you first must puppet the sprite. Then you can use Lingo to move the sprite around. In this chapter, we made the location of the sprite equal to the position of the cursor. You can also set the location of sprites through keystrokes.

Director can detect when sprites intersect or when sprites are within other sprites. You can then program Director to take certain actions based on the placement of sprites on the stage. Director can also detect when a sound is playing in a particular channel of the score and react, depending on whether or not a sound is playing.

You have seen how to combine all this to create a game-style learning tool. This chapter has just scratched the surface of what you can create using Lingo to manipulate the placement of sprites. Now it's your turn to use these tools you have learned to your advantage.

CHAPTER 10

USING XTRAS

Lingo included in this chapter:

```
showXlib
mMessageList
new(Xtra XtraName)
displaySave(instance, string title, string defaultFileName)
openFile(instance, string fileName, int openMode)
setFinderInfo(instance, "FileType Creator")
CreateFile(instance, string fileName)
writeString(instance, string)
closeFile(instance)
put error(instance, status(instance))
setTextFont printInfo, font
setTextSize printInfo, size
append
doJobSetUp
setLandscapeMode
```

As powerful as Director is, there will be times when you want it to do something it is not programmed to do. That doesn't mean that you must abandon Director completely and go learn C++ or Visual Basic. Chances are that whatever it is you want to do, it can be accomplished with Lingo Xtras or their predecessors, XObjects. Xtras and XObjects are bits of code that add to Director's functionality. You can develop your own Xtras or use someone else's. There are many third parties that create Xtras for Director. Xtras that are currently available give you greater printing capabilities, allow you to record and play back sound from kiosks, allow you to manage databases, let you search, sort, and replace text, and let you incorporate speech recognition, just to name a few.

Xtras can be a little tricky to use because they are not actually created with Lingo but created in computer languages such as C, Pascal, or assembly language. Lingo is based on English, so it is not difficult to learn and use, while these other programming languages follow grammar and/or syntax rules that you may not be familiar with.

Every Xtra has its own documentation and its own set of commands. In this chapter, you will learn how to use the FileIO Xtra and the PrintOMatic Lite Xtra that come with Director 5.0.

The version of FileIO Xtra that ships with Director 5.0 is a beta version, meaning that it is not the finished version and could be a little buggy or missing some commands that will be added to a later version. For the most up-to-date version of FileIO Xtra, check out Macromedia's web site at www.macromedia.com.

What is FileIO?

Imagine that you developed a kiosk. Wouldn't it be handy if users could input their names, addresses, and requests for additional information and Director saved them for you in a text file? You would have a custom-made customer list! What if your application could read information on a hard drive and display different content depending on what the user wanted to see? Director itself will not support reading or writing text files. However, you can do all these things with the *FileIO* Xtra.

FileIO stands for File Input Output.

Getting Started

Before you play the example movie, you must make sure the FileIO Xtra is in the Director Xtras folder or directory. You also need the FileSupport Xtra in the same location. On the Macintosh, the FileSupport Xtra is just called **FileSupportXtra**. The name varies on Windows. If you are using Windows 95 or Windows NT, use the **FILESUPT.X32**. If you are using Windows 3.1, use the **FILESUPT.X16**. Once both the FileIO Xtra and the FileSupport Xtra are located in the proper location, you can open the movie **FileIcom.dir**.

There is an easy way to determine if you have the FileIO Xtra. Open the Message window within Director and type:

```
showXlib
```

Press the **Return** key, and the Message window will list all the Lingo Xtras Director was able to locate (see Figure 10.1).

Figure 10.1 Lingo Xtras and XObjects located by Director.

If you can't find the FileIO Xtra or its support Xtra, you can download it from the Macromedia Web site for free.

NOTE

Play the movie. Type anything you want on the stage. To save it, click the **Save** button. Director gives you the option of what to name your file and where to save it (see Figure 10.2). On Windows, it also gives you the option of what type of file you want.

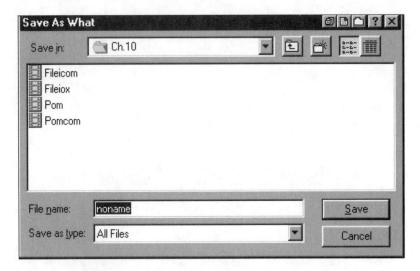

Figure 10.2 Save dialog box for Windows 95.

Type in a name and choose a location. Click **Save**.

Stop the movie. Look in whatever place you chose to save it. Double-click on the file. It opens up as a text document. There it is! Director took your text and wrote it to an external text file. Go back to Director. Take a look at the Score and Cast windows. The entire movie consists of only one frame and four cast members. The cast member on the stage that is holding your text is a field cast member (Figure 10.3).

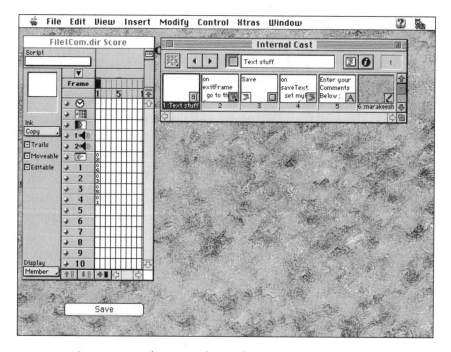

Figure 10.3 The cast and score for the movie **FileIcomdir**.

Creating an Instance of the Xtra

Open the movie **FileIOX.dir** on the CD that accompanies this book. You want the FileIO Xtra to do its thing when you click the **Save** button. Because this button is always going to do the same thing, you can use a cast member script to activate the Xtra.

Select the **Save** button in the Cast window. Click the **Script** button. You will place a handler name in here and create the handler in the Movie window. Create the following handler:

```
on mouseUp
      saveText
end
```

SaveText is a user-defined handler. You need to create it in the movie script. Close the Script window and open your movie script.

The first thing you need to do to use an Xtra is create an instance of the Xtra. Think of the Xtra as a cookie cutter. The cookie created by the cutter is the instance. After the cookie has been cut out by the cutter, you can customize the cookie any way you want. You could decorate it or add nuts to it or whatever you wanted. When you create an instance of an Xtra, you then need to use additional code for it to behave exactly as you want it to.

Each Lingo Xtra has its own list of commands, functions, and properties. The commands and functions associated with an Xtra are called *methods*. You can think of a method as a handler, except in this case, you don't actually see all the lines of code that make up the handler. You can find all the methods and parameters associated with the FileIO Xtra (Figure 10.4) by typing the following in the Message window:

```
put mMessageList(Xtra "fileIO")
```

In this chapter, you will use several of these methods to place the text that the user has inputted in a Director movie into an external text file. Create the following handler in the movie script:

```
on saveText
     set myText=new(xtra "fileIO")
end
```

You have just created a single instance of the fileIO Xtra and given it a name. You name the instance because you can have use than one instance at the same time. If you wanted to read more than one file at once or write to more than one file at a time or a combination of both, you need to have a separate instance of fileIO for each file you are working with.

Next you will put the contents of the editable field cast member into a variable.

Add the following line to your handler:

```
put field "text stuff" into StoreIt
```

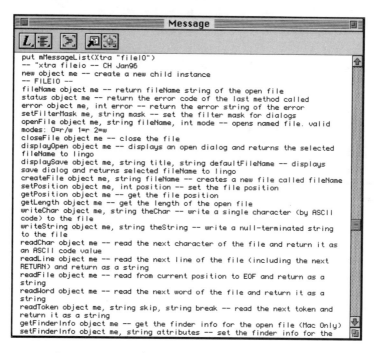

Figure 10.4 Methods associated with the FileIO Xtra.

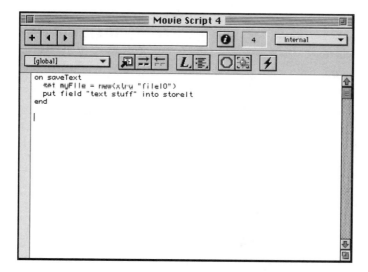

Figure 10.5 Your movie handler for the movie **FileIOX.dir**.

StoreIt is a local variable you just created.

Displaying a Save Dialog Box

Next, to give your user the ability to choose the title of his or her file and the location in which to store it, you will use the **displaySave** command. The command looks like:

```
displaySave(instance, string title, string defaultFileName)
```

What does all that mean? It means that you want to display a Save dialog box with specific attributes. When you save documents in a word processor, the dialog box usually says, "Save As" above the box in which you enter the name of the file. When using the FileIO Xtra, you can customize what you want the dialog box to say. Also, you can specify the default name of the file. Usually you see the default name "untitled." You may choose to use a more unique default file name. Last, you can store the displaySave string in a variable.

Under the put field "text stuff" into storeIt line, add the following code:

```
set whatFile=displaySave(myText, "Save as What?", "noname")
```

Now, you will be displaying a dialog box (Figure 10.6) that will say "Save as What?" with the default name "noname." The variable whatFile is capturing the location and name of the file the user is creating.

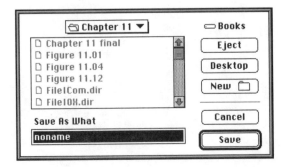

Figure 10.6 Your Save dialog box.

Creating a New File

Now you need to tell FileIO to create the file as defined by the user with the **CreateFile**(instance, string fileName) command. In this case, you don't know exactly what the filename is going to be. That is OK because you have the file name stored in the whatFile variable. Add the following line to the handler:

```
CreateFile(myText, whatFile)
```

Once a file is created, you still need the Xtra to open it so it can place the text inside it. The user will not see the text file open because the Xtra is opening the file internally.

Getting Ready to Save Text

The code to open the file looks like:

```
openFile(instance, string fileName, int openMode)
```

The int openMode parameter tells the Xtra whether you are using this Xtra to read a file, write to a file, or both. To read a file, the openMode=1; to write to a file, the openMode=2. To do both, the openMode=0. In this case, you want to write to a file. Place the following line in your saveText handler:

```
openFile(myText, whatFile, 2)
```

Compare your movie script with the one in Figure 10.7.

File Types

If you are using a Windows computer, the file will automatically be saved as a text file. In fact, on Windows 95, when the user defines the name of the file and its location, the dialog box that appears (Figure 10.8) also allows the user to change the file type from text to anything else they want.

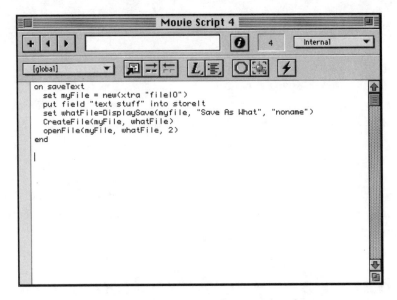

Figure 10.7 Your movie script for using the FileIO Xtra.

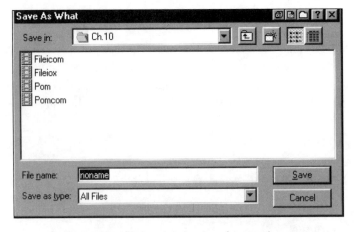

Figure 10.8 The Save dialog box for Windows 95.

On Windows 3.1, the file type is dependent on the three-character extension you place in the file name. On Macintosh, it's a little more complicated. You will need to add an additional line of code.

If you are using a Macintosh, you will need to add a line after the **openFile** command to define what type of file will be used to save the text. The line looks like:

```
setFinderInfo(instance, "FileType Creator")
```

The file type and creator are always indicated by four characters each. So if you wanted a TeachText or SimpleText document, the code would be:

```
setFinderInfo(MyText, "TEXT ttxt")
```

The type and creator are case-sensitive. Text will always be in all caps. If you want a Microsoft Word document, the code will be:

```
setFinderInfo(MyText, "TEXT MSWD")
```

Both the file type and the creator on the Macintosh are four letters long. Figure 10.9 gives you some types and creators for different applications.

Application	Type	Creator
WordPerfect text file	TEXT	WPC2
ClarisWorks text file	sWWP	BOBO
Excel spreadsheet	APPL	XCEL
Photoshop text file	TEXT	8BIM
ReadMe	TEXT	stxt
Acrobat Reader (read only)	ttro	CARO
MacWrite Pro	TEXT	MWPR
Nisus Writer	TEXT	NISI

Figure 10.9 Type and creator for select applications.

Writing to a Text File

Finally, you are ready to tell the Xtra to write to the new file. The **write** command is:

```
writeString(instance, string)
```

Add the following line to your handler:

```
writeString(MyText, storeIt)
```

Remember that storeIt is the local variable that contains the text from the field cast member.

Cleaning Up

Now that the Xtra has done its job, you need to do a little cleaning. First, you want to close the file that was opened to place the text in. Next, you want to remove the instance of the Xtra you created out of memory. Then you will be ready to try it out.

Place the following two lines at the end of your handler (see Figure 10.10):

```
closeFile(myText)
set myText=0
```

Close your movie script and play the movie. Type some text on the screen and click the **Save** button. Then choose a name for your file and a location in which to save it. Now stop your movie. Finally, locate your newly created file and open it. Your text is now in the file.

If you start your movie again, you will see that the old text you typed is still on the stage. It is better if every time you start the movie, the field cast member is empty. Adding a stopMovie handler will accomplish this.

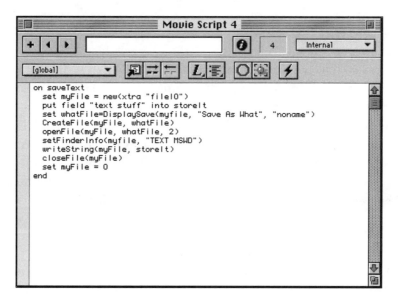

Figure 10.10 The finished *saveText* handler.

 NOTE You are using a *stopMovie* handler instead of a *startMovie* handler here because the *startMovie* handler would delay the start of the movie. While the delay would not be noticeable here because you are just clearing one field, the delay does become noticeable once you have a few lines of code in the *startMovie* handler.

Open your movie script and add the following handler:

```
on stopMovie
    put "" into field "text stuff"
end
```

"Text stuff" is the name of the field cast member that stores the user's text. Now, every time the movie is stopped, the field is cleared.

Debugging Tips

There are two other commands you can use with the FileIO Xtra that will help you debug it. They are **error**(instance, integer error) and **status**(instance). **Status** will give you an error code for the most recent operation while **error** will give you an actual readable error string such as "OK," "Bad File Name," "File Not Open," or "File Not Found." Since the **error** command requires a numeric error code and **status** generates a numeric error code, you can use these two commands in conjunction to give you the exact type of problem. To use them, place the following line within your *saveText* handler:

```
put error(myText, status(myText))
```

To find out exactly where the error is occurring, place this line after every command line in the handler. Your handler will look like this:

```
on saveText
    set myText = new(xtra "fileIO")
    put field "text stuff" into storeIt
    set whatFile=DisplaySave(myText , "Save As What", "noname")
    put error(myText, status(myText))
    CreateFile(myFile, whatFile)
    put error(myText, status(myText))
    openFile(myFile, whatFile, 2)
    put error(myText, status(myText))
    writeString(myFile, storeIt)
    put error(myText, status(myText))
    closeFile(myFile)
    put error(myText, status(myText))
    set myFile = 0
end
```

To see the results of these error-catching lines, close the movie script, play the movie, enter some text, and click the **Save** button. Stop your movie and open your Message window. You will see the results of the put error line. If you want to be able to see quickly where the movie is breaking down, click the **Trace** button in the Message window before playing your movie (see Figure 10.11). Then you can see exactly where the handler is breaking down.

Figure 10.11 Tracing your handler with the Message window.

Once you are finished tracing your handler, you will want to delete the put error lines from your code.

PrintOMatic Lite

The next Xtra you'll explore is called PrintOMatic Lite. If you have ever tried to print text on the stage while a movie is playing, you have a couple of options. You can either try printing out the anti-aliased text, resulting in ugly bitmapped printout or you can print text that is not anti-aliased at the same size as it is on the stage. The printout looks cleaner but is usually much bigger than is necessary for print. Neither option is great. Luckily, there is a third option, which is to use the PrintOMatic Xtra. PrintOMatic Lite ships with Director 5.0. With PrintOMatic Lite, you can print cast members, sprites, cast Libraries, or customized documents. You can change the style of the strings, set document names, and print in landscape mode. In this exercise, you will set the font you wish to print, its size, and the orientation of the paper.

NOTE   Before you start this exercise, make sure the Xtra is in the Director Xtras folder or directory.

Getting Started

Open the movie **POMCom.dir** on the CD accompanying this book. Play the movie. Type in your information on the stage. You can use the **Tab** key to move from one field to another. When you are finished, click the **Print** button. You will see the Print dialog box for your printer. Click **OK**. Check your printout. The printout is a different font and size than the text on the stage. Stop the movie. In the Message window, type:

```
put mMessageList(Xtra "PrintOMatic_Lite")
```

and press the **Return** key. Take a look at all the methods and parameters associated with this Xtra (Figure 10.12). These give you a good idea as to what you can accomplish with the PrintOMatic Lite Xtra.

```
Message
L  E  E  E  E

put mMessageList(Xtra "Printomatic_lite")
-- "xtra PrintOMatic_Lite
--
-- PrintOMatic Lite Xtra
-- Version 1.5.1
-- Copyright 1994-96 Electronic Ink
--
-- CREATE/DESTROY/RESET A DOCUMENT
new object
forget object
reset object
--
-- DOCUMENT PRINTING SETUP
doPageSetup object
doJobSetup object
setLandscapeMode object, boolean
setMargins object, rect
setDocumentName object, string
--
-- TEXT ATTRIBUTES
setTextFont object, string
setTextSize object, int
setTextStyle object, string
--
-- APPEND TO DOCUMENT
append object, *
--
-- PRINTING
printPreview object
* print *
"
```

Figure 10.12 Methods and parameters for PrintOMatic Lite Xtra.

Creating an Instance for PrintOMatic Lite

Open the movie **POM.dir**. The **Print** button already has a cast member script attached to it. It looks like:

```
on mouseUp
      PrintText
end
```

Look at the score (Figure 10.13). You have some text cast members and some field cast members. The user types his or her information in the field cast members. These field cast members are titled according to the information they will contain.

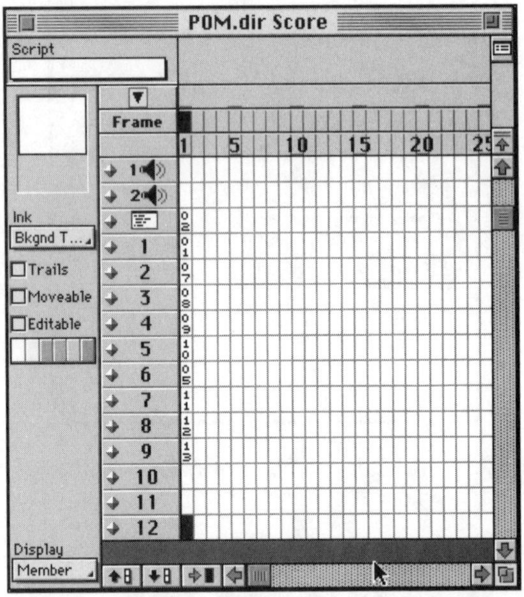

Figure 10.13 The score for the movie **POM.dir**.

Look at the Cast window. The field members that are storing the user's information are all named. You will use those names later in your movie script. The **Print** button already has a script attached to it that is calling the *PrintText* handler. However, the *PrintText* handler does not exist; you will create it now in the movie script.

Open your movie script.

The first thing you need to do when using an Xtra is create an instance of it. Create instances that are similar for all Xtras. Create the following handler:

```
on PrintText
    set printInfo=new(xtra "PrintOMatic_Lite")
end
```

An instance of PrintOMatic Lite Xtra is called a *document object*. You have just created a document object called printInfo.

Next, you will choose the font you want to use for your document object. Choose a font that is currently in your system and that you know will print out nicely. If you are creating something like this for distribution, make sure you use a font that is common to most computers. If you are going to distribute it cross-platform, be careful about what font you choose. Also, you will indicate to Director at what size you want the font to print out.

 Times Roman size 12 on the Macintosh and Times Roman size 12 on Windows are not the same size. Make sure you do not crowd the text you want to print with a tight border or other objects unless you have tested your layout on both platforms and found it to be satisfactory.

NOTE

Add the following lines to your handler before the *end* keyword:

```
setTextFont printInfo, "Times"
setTextSize printInfo, 12
```

PrintOMatic does not actually format field cast members or rich text cast members. It formats text strings so you can't ask it to format a cast member, but you can place the contents of a cast member into a variable and then format the variable. You want to format the contents of "NameText," "AddressText," and "CityText." The best way to do this is to combine the contents of those three cast members into a single variable. You can use the operator "&" to place all the cast members into one variable. The ampersand (&) is a concatenator. To *concatenate* two items means to put them together (Figure 10.14). If you typed the following expression into the Message window:

```
put "meat" & "ball"
```

the Message window would return:

```
"meatball"
```

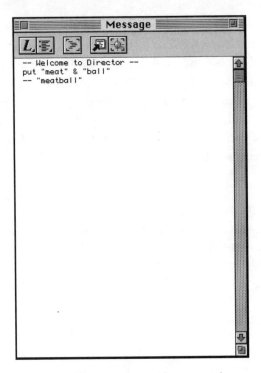

Figure 10.14 Using the Message window to test the concatenator.

There is a second concatenator (&&) that will also put things together but will leave a space between the two text strings.

NOTE

You will use the concatenator to combine the three text strings into a single variable. As the next line of your handler, type:

```
set PrintAll=field "nametext"&RETURN&field¬
"addressText"&RETURN&"field "CityText"
```

See Figure 10.15 for a view of the *printText* handler in the movie script.

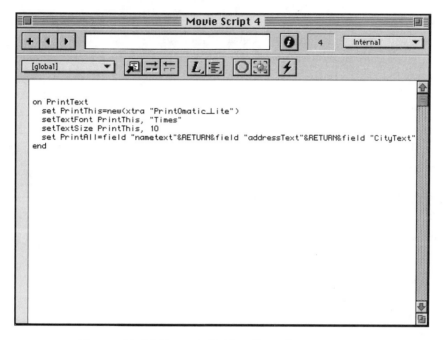

Figure 10.15 Your *printText* handler in the movie script.

The word RETURN is there to separate each field onto a new line of the text document.

N O T E If you wanted to use commas so that this text can easily be imported into a database, the line would look like:

```
set PrintAll=field "nametext"&","&field
"addressText"&","&field "CityText"
```

Next, you tell Director what you want to have printed with the font and size attributes you assigned earlier. This is known as *appending* items to the document object. Add the following line before the *end* statement of your *printText* handler:

```
append PrintText, PrintAll
```

So that the user can choose certain attributes of his or her own particular printer, you will show them the Print Options modal dialog box. This is the same box they would normally find if they chose **Print** from the File menu in Director. The code to do this looks like:

```
if doJobSetUp (instance) then print instance
```

Placing your instance name in the preceding line gives you the code you need to print the information. Add the following line to your handler:

```
if doJobSetUp (PrintText) then print printText
```

You are almost done! One more line to go! After you have used an instance of an Xtra, you want to remove that instance because they take up memory. To dispose of the PrintOMatic Lite Xtra, set your instance equal to **0**.

```
set PrintText=0
```

And that will do it (see Figure 10.16).

Close the movie handler and rewind and play your movie. Type some information on the screen and then click the **Print** button. Your information comes out on the page in smaller text and a different font than you saw on the screen.

To clear the text the user typed on the screen the next time someone plays this movie, you can add a simple stopMovie handler. This will make the movie look neat and clean.

Now stop your movie and open your movie script. At the bottom of the Script window add the following handler:

```
on stopMovie
    put "" into field "nameText"
    put "" into field "addressText"
    put "" into field "cityText"
end
```

This script will clean out whatever was typed in the field cast members, making them ready for new information.

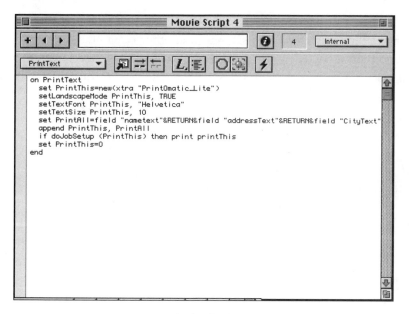

Figure 10.16 the finished *printText* handler.

If you need to print in landscape mode, PrintOMatic Lite will do that for you too. Use the following command:

```
setLandscapeMode instance, TRUE
```

NOTE

Summary

Xtras give you additional functionality beyond what Director was created to do. They can do a variety of things for you, from accessing databases to creating pop-up menus within your application. Many third-party vendors are developing Xtras. There is a good chance that if you need to expand Director's functionality, there is already an Xtra created that will do what you need done. To investigate the type of Lingo Xtras that are out there, visit Macromedia's Web site. The list of Lingo Xtras is growing daily.

Xtras are not as easy to use as plain old Lingo, but they are worth looking into. Each Xtra is going to have its own unique commands and attributes that you will need to master to use them effectively. However, it is still better than creating the functionality from scratch in another computer language. If you can't find the functionality you need in the Xtras already developed, the Xtras Developer's Kit ships with Director 5.0 if you feel adventurous enough to build your own.

CHAPTER 11

SHOCKWAVE GOODIES

Lingo included in this chapter:

```
gotoNetMovie
preLoadNetThing
gotoNetPage
StartTimer
soundBusy
keyDown
mouseDown
netDone()
```

Have you logged onto the Internet, seen an animation with music on a page and wondered how it is done? You can do it too using your own Director movies! It doesn't even take any fancy techniques or additional software purchases. This chapter gives hints on how to optimize your movie for playback on the World Wide Web, how to create a "shocked" movie, how to embed it on a page using HTML (Hypertext Markup Language), and some Lingo workarounds for score options that are not available in Shockwave movies.

What is Shockwave?

Shockwave is an exciting new technology that allows you to play your Director movies on the World Wide Web. The movies download just like any other graphic and then play as soon as the downloading is completed. During the downloading process, the user sees a gray box with the Macromedia logo in it.

Director's Shockwave technology contains two parts: the Afterburner and the Shockwave plug-in. The plug-in allows you to view Shockwave movies on a Web page using your Internet browser. The afterburner is a postprocessor for Director movies that compresses the movie and makes it ready to be loaded onto the Web. A movie must be "shocked" in order for it to be used on the Web. After a movie has gone through the Afterburner, it will have the extension **.dcr**. Both of these parts are available free at Macromedia's Web site (www.macromedia.com). Be careful when downloading these two elements. Both are platform-specific. If you are authoring in a Mac environment, make sure you use the Afterburner for the Macintosh. Also, to view Shockwave movies with your net browser, you need the proper plug-in for your operating system and your Net browser.

NOTE   Even though the Afterburner is platform specific, the shocked movie is not. It can be viewed on any platform as long as the user has the proper Shockwave plug-in.

All you need to do to shock your Director movie is to run it through the Afterburner. Make sure the Afterburner plug-in is located in your Xtras folder. Next, open the movie you want to shock. Then, from the Xtras menu, select MacroTools and the submenu item Afterburner. The movie is automatically shocked, compressing it approximately 50% and ready to be placed on your web site.

NOTE   After a movie is shocked, the shocked movie cannot be edited, so never discard the original Director movie.

What You Can't Do with Shockwave

You should be aware that certain Lingo commands are not supported in a Shockwave movie. Most of them have to do with issues of security on the Internet. For example, you cannot use the commands **Quit**, **Restart**, or **Shutdown**. Imagine if you were minding your own business, looking at some-one's Web page, and when the Shockwave movie ended, your computer turned off! Chances are you would not be very happy. Also not available are the commands **Open Window** and **Close Window**. That means you cannot use Movies in a Window on the 'net. There are a few other less frequently used commands not available with Shockwave. For an entire list of Lingo disabled for Shockwave, refer to Macromedia's Shockwave Developers Center at www.macromedia.com/Tools/Shockwave/sdc/dev.

One other thing that is more likely to cause you problems is the fact that the Tempo channel is not supported with Shockwave, which means no Tempo changes, no "wait for mouse Click or Keypress," no "wait for Sound1 to Finish," etc. The good news is that all these things can be accomplished with some simple Lingo scripts.

Working Around Shockwave's Limitations

Creating a Delay

Because you cannot use the Tempo channel to create a delay, you can implement this simple Lingo script. This script is handy for many tasks, not just in a Shockwave movie. It can be used in a frame script, movie script, or sprite or cast member script. In this example, the frame script is creating a 1-second delay.

```
on enterFrame
    startTimer
    repeat while the timer < 60
        nothing
    end repeat
end
```

Director has an internal stopwatch that is always running when a movie is playing. Director is constantly keeping track of certain events like the last time the mouse button was clicked (lastClick) or how long it has been since a key was pressed (lastKey). Director counts in ticks with 60 ticks in a second. *StartTimer* is a Lingo command that resets Director's timer property. You want to reset it back to zero so you can count out 1 second starting from zero. The repeat loop tells Director to keep doing the commands within the repeat loop for 1 second. The command within the repeat loop tells Director to do nothing! Believe it or not, *nothing* is a legal Lingo command. After 60 ticks have passed, the playback head will move again.

You can use this simple script in a variety of ways. If you want the playback head to branch after a 1-second delay, add a **go to** command after the delay.

```
on exitFrame
    startTimer
    repeat while the timer < 60
        nothing
    end repeat
    go to "freedom"
end
```

The playback head will remain in the current frame for 1 second before branching to the label "freedom."

To cut down on tedious calculations, you can also have Director calculate how many ticks are in the amount of seconds you want in your delay.

```
repeat while the timer < 60* (number of seconds)
```

If you wanted a 5- second delay, the repeat code would be:

```
repeat while the timer < 60 * 5
```

You can re-use this script for different amounts of time by placing it in the movie script and an argument in the repeat line.

```
on wait whatTime
    startTimer
```

```
        repeat while the timer < whatTime
            nothing
        end repeat
end
```

In the handler where you need a delay, call the wait handler and specify how long you want the delay for. You can call this wait handler from any type of script. If you need a 2-second delay when a sprite is clicked, the sprite script will look like:

```
on mouseUp
        wait (2*60)
end
```

Waiting for a Sound to Finish

Because you cannot use the command **Wait for Sound to Finish** in the Tempo channel, here is a script to help you:

```
on exitFrame
        if soundBusy (1) then go to the frame
end
```

What this is saying is, if there is a sound playing in sound channel 1, then stay where you are. If the sound isn't playing, move to the next frame. This script can be modified to work for a sound playing in sound channel 2. Substitute a 2 within the parentheses and it's ready to go.

Another time you may need a delay is when using puppetSounds. If you need to play a puppetSound and then turn off puppetSounds within the same handler, it is possible that the **puppetSound 0** command will be issued before the entire puppetSound has time to play. In that case, you can call the preceding delay handler to give the puppetSound a little more time to finish, then the **puppetSound 0** command is issued, returning control of sound channel 1 back to the score (see Chapter 8).

Waiting for a Mouse Click or Key

You may think this is difficult to do with Lingo, but it's actually very simple. The following three scripts all need to reside together in a frame script in order to work:

```
on exitFrame
     go to the frame
end

on mouseDown
     go to the frame + 1
end

on keyDown
     go to the frame +1
end
```

With these scripts in a frame script, your movie will stay in the same frame until someone clicks the mouse button or presses a key. Then it will go to the next frame. You can modify this script to branch anywhere you want. Also, this movie could branch to two different locations depending on whether the mouse is clicked or a key is pressed.

Wait for QuickTime in Channel X to be Finished

Currently, you cannot have any linked media in a Shockwave movie. That has to do with the problems of a networked environment. After your shocked movie has downloaded, it is possible that network traffic could prevent retrieval of the linked media. Also the size of QuickTime movies tends to be rather large. The name of the game with Shockwave is to make it as small as possible. If your QuickTime movie is small, you can output it as a series of PICS and use those in a Director movie. For more information on QuickTime in a Shockwave movie, refer to Macromedia's Web site.

The *Major* Consideration: Size

The main issue when creating a shocked movie is its size. You want to make it as small as possible. Because the entire movie will automatically download when you reach a page with a Shockwave movie and most people surfing the net have 14.4K baud modems, you need to make your movie as small as possible to cut down on download times (see Figure 11.1). Even a 500Kb movie can take 5 minutes or longer to download on a 28.8Kb modem due to traffic on the Internet and network congestion. A few simple ways to make your movie small is to use 1-bit color cast members wherever possible, use Tiles to create patterned backgrounds, and use the Tools palette for shapes. These three easy techniques will significantly reduce the size of your movie. Keep the users in mind. Will they be willing to wait 5 minutes or longer to see your Shockwave movie or will they have already moved on to a new site?

Typical Download Times

Size/Speed	14.4kbs	28.8kbs	64kbs	1.5mbps
30K	30 sec	10 sec	6 sec	1 sec
100–200K	3–5 min	1.5–3 min	20–40 sec	1 sec
500K	4–8 min	2–4 min	1.5 min	3 sec
1 Meg	13.3–26.7 min	6.7–13.7 min	3 min	6 sec

Figure 11.1 Typical download times for Shockwave movies of various sizes.

New Lingo Exclusively for Shockwave

Macromedia has created some new Lingo for use with the Internet. Interestingly enough, these new Lingo elements are not in the Lingo Dictionary that ships with Director. You can find all the new Lingo at the Macromedia Web site, or just keep reading!

Downloading a Second Movie

Here's a little trick you can use if you need to use a large movie. Create a smaller movie and have that downloaded first. Then use Lingo to download the bigger movie. The first movie will continue to play until the new movie has completely downloaded and is ready to play. Within the first movie, use the following command:

```
gotoNetMovie URL.
```

You can use this in a *startMovie* handler or in any other kind of script. If you place it in the *startMovie* handler, as soon as the smaller first movie starts to play, the second movie will begin to download. When the second movie has been downloaded, the first movie will stop without warning and the second movie will take its place. The second movie will play in the same position on the page as the first movie. For that reason, make sure that the stage size for the second movie is not bigger than the stage of the first one. If it is bigger, it will be cropped to fit the space occupied by the first movie.

The URL (Uniform Resource Locator) can be either a filename or an anchor within a file so your URL will look something like:

```
http://www.yourserver.com/movies/moviename.dcr
```

Using this URL as an example, your *startMovie* handler would look like:

```
on startMovie
      gotoNetMovie "http://www.yourserver.com/movies/moviename.dcr"
end
```

Using Shockwave for Navigation

The most exciting use of Shockwave is for navigation. You have seen how you can navigate to different parts of a movie using Lingo. Now you can navigate to different pages on the Internet using Lingo! A great example of this can be found at www.oddo.com, the home page for Oddo Design in Houston, Texas (Figure 11.2).

Figure 11.2 Oddo Design's Shockwave movie.

Many of the scripts mentioned earlier as workarounds can also be found in this movie. Take the time to investigate all the scripts in the movie **Shokroom.dir**.

N O T E

As you enter the page, you are welcomed by a Shockwave movie emulating the offices of Oddo Design complete with office chatter in the background. Clicking on the television screen will give you oodles of options for how to proceed. Do you want to see a company profile? A list of awards they have won? A client list? Samples? Job opportunities? (See Figure 11.3.)

Figure 11.3 Using a Shockwave movie for navigation.

All these options are hot links to other Web pages within the Oddo site. Not only can you use the TV screen for navigation, you can click on virtually anything within the office setting and be instantly transported to another page.

This movie is included on the CD that accompanies this book, so you can see how it was built. This version has been altered to emulate what it would look like on the Web. The first four links on the television screen will bring you to screen shots of the Web pages they would navigate to. Clicking the **Back** button will return you to the main screen.

If you click the next button on the bottom of the screen, you will see more navigation. This navigation was left alone; if you click on one of those links, you will get an error because the Director movie is trying to find a Web page (see Figure 11.4).

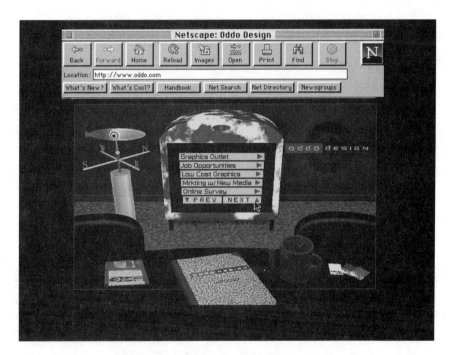

Figure 11.4 Screen of links "as is."

This navigation was left alone so that you could see what the scripts look like and how to create a great "shocked" movie. To really get a feel for how powerful this movie is, visit Oddo's Web site to see this movie, or one similar to it, in action.

The Lingo that allows you to branch to different Web pages is:

```
gotoNetPage URL
```

In the case of Oddo Design's movie **shokroom.dir**, the above Lingo was placed in a sprite script. The entire script is:

```
on mouseUp
    gotoNetPage "http://oddo.com/profile.html"
end
```

That's it! It's nothing fancy or complex, but it sure is powerful.

Preloading on the Web

Another way to use a Shockwave movie is to entertain while downloading larger files. For example, when the user goes to a new page, you can play a Shockwave movie while preloading a graphic. That way, the user does not feel like he is wasting time while the graphic is loading. For this to work, you need to place the Shockwave movie at the top of your page and have the graphic lower on the page or on a subsequent page. The Lingo that will preload a graphic, movie, or another page is:

```
preloadNetThing URL
```

This command loads whatever you specify into the browser disk cache so that it can be used later without a download delay. Your Shockwave movie will play while the preloading takes place. Once your item is preloaded, it can be used immediately. Keep in mind, though, that you don't know when the item may be dumped out of the disk cache, so don't use this command unless you know for sure the item is going to be used, and don't use this command too far in advance.

There is one other piece of Lingo created for use with the World Wide Web that you may find useful: *netDone()*. This function returns a value of 1 or 0. It will tell you whether a preloadNetThing is done. If netDone() returns a value of 1, then the item is finished preloading and is ready to view. If netDone() is 0, then Director is still preloading your item.

One thing that is tricky with this command is that it will also return a value of 1 if the preLoadNetThing operation has been terminated by a browser error.

N O T E

Let's say, for example, you want to preload the next page of your Web site. You want a Shockwave movie to play until the new page is in place. You could use netDone in a frame script. If the page is still preloading, the movie will play again. If the preloading is finished, you will go to the page you just preloaded. In the last frame of the movie, place a frame script that reads:

```
on exitFrame
    if netDone()=TRUE then
        gotoNetPage "http://www.yourserver.com/your homepage"
    else
        go to "start"
    end if
end
```

The Internet is an asynchronous environment. You cannot depend on a constant rate of downloading. There are so many variables that you cannot control, such as the amount of users online and the speed of a user's modem. Having a command like **netDone()** available allows you to work around the fact that you cannot create a movie of a specific length to occupy your user while your next page is downloading.

Shockwave and HTML

So now you've created your Director movie, added Web navigation, "shocked" it with the afterburner, and are ready to put it on your Web page. Now what do you do? All you need is one HTML command to place it on your page. You need to use the <EMBED> tag along with the location of the movie and the movie's dimensions. It looks like this:

```
<EMBED SRC="path/filename.ext" WIDTH=n HEIGHT=m>
```

If your movie is called *peanuts* and the stage size is 320 by 240 pixels, your code would look like:

```
<Embed SRC="http://www.yourserver.com/movies/peanuts.dcr"
WIDTH=320¬ HEIGHT=240>
```

If you specify dimensions that are smaller than your stage, the movie will be cropped not scaled down to fit the size you indicate within the EMBED tag.

Another aspect of your movie that you can qualify when embedding it is its palette. You can either use the palette that is in your Director movie or use the system palette on the user's computer. Computers can only use one palette at a time so if you force the movie to use its palette, the rest of the monitor will have to use it as well. This means that your user could get some very unusual special effects you did not intend to give them! It is best to use the system palette for your Shockwave movies. In fact, using the system palette is the default for the **EMBED** command. If you do want to make sure your Shockwave movie plays with its own palette, add the argument PALETTE=foreground after the movie's dimensions. The argument PALETTE=background will prevent the palette within the movie from being loaded.

Substitutions?

Although it is Macromedia's intention to distribute a Shockwave plug-in for every Web browser out there, it is still possible that a user will not have the plug-in. Because of this, you may want to substitute a graphic (Figure 11.6) for your Shockwave movie. You can do this with the <NOEMBED> tag. That way, the user will get some type of visual instead of a broken link icon. For example:

```
<NOEMBED>
<IMG SRC=""http://www.yourserver.com/images/peanuts.GIF">
</NOEMBED>
```

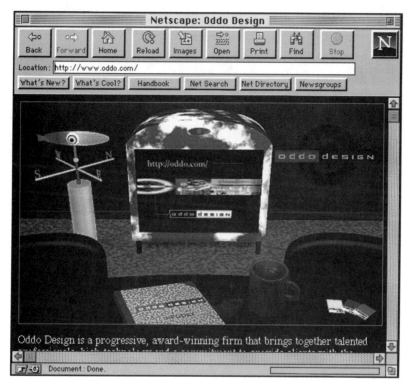

Figure 11.5 Substitute graphic for **oddo.com** Web site.

Summary

With the Internet booming as it is, it's an exciting time to be in multimedia. The Internet is turning into a great marketing device, a practical way to get an education, and a novel way to meet new people! Imagine how people will flock to your site once your cool Shockwave movie is up and running. You now have the tools you need to create ground-breaking animation on your Web site.

Using Shockwave for navigation makes it fun to "surf" a Web site. It makes a page memorable. It gets rid of the tedium of clicking on page after page of text to get to where you want to go. Using Shockwave as a diversion while other movies or pages are loading is a good way to keep the user at your site even when it is necessary to download larger items. With more and more sites appearing daily, using Shockwave can give you that competitive edge.

When creating a Shockwave movie, remember to make the movie as small as possible. Use 1-bit cast members where possible. Use tiling for backgrounds. Use the Tools palette whenever possible for shapes. Once you have created your movie, you can use Macromedia's "DownloadOMatic" located at Macromedia's Web site to find out how long it will take for your shocked movie to download.

Shockwave is a new technology. It is growing and evolving constantly. To keep up to date on all the new Lingo being created for it as well as sites that are "shocked," visit Macromedia's Web site at www.macromedia.com.

GLOSSARY

Afterburner   The Director 5.0 Xtra that creates a Shockwave movie from your Director movie that you can place on your Web page. A Director movie that has been "shocked" has the extension **.dcr**.

AIFF   A sound file format that can be used on both Mac and Windows. AIFF stands for Audio Interchange File Format.

argument   A variable whose value is passed from other scripts as needed.

concatenator (&)   Something that adds items together. In Lingo, concatenators most often join strings of characters.

function   A Lingo function returns a value.

handler   A group of lines of Lingo code. A handler always begins with the word *on* and ends with the word *end*.

HTML   The language most commonly used to create pages for the Internet. HTML stands for Hypertext Markup Language.

human interface guidelines   A set of platform-specific guidelines for computer applications to adhere to. An example is how pull-down menus behave. Windows programs that follow human interface guidelines display the menu items when the user clicks on a menu name. On the Mac, the user must click and hold down the mouse key to see the menu items. By following human interface guidelines in your applications, users will have a good idea of how to use the application.

label   The alphanumeric name attached to a marker in the score.

Lingo   The programming language created for Director by John Thompson.

MIAW   Movie in a Window; MIAW is a way to play more than one Director movie at a time.

puppet   An element of a movie that obeys Lingo instead of the score. The most common puppet is a puppetSprite. PuppetSprites are used in creating sophisticated buttons. PuppetSounds, puppetTempos, and puppetTransitions are also possible.

Shockwave   A new way to package and play Director movies on the Internet. The movie plays directly on a Web page. The two parts of Shockwave are the post-processor for Director movies, called the *Afterburner*, and the Shockwave plug-in that allows your browser to interpret the movie and play it back on the Web page.

sprite   An instance of a castmember in the score. Think of an actor backstage of a play; he is just himself. When he steps onto the stage, he takes on a role, where he may speak or stand differently. When a castmember is on the stage, it is called a *sprite*. The sprite can be bigger or smaller than the castmember. In some cases, the sprite can be a different color. The castmember keeps its original characteristics.

APPENDIX A

Lingo included in this appendix:

```
the cursor of sprite
sound playFile
case
freeBytes
ramNeeded
pathName
alert
```

There are so many exciting things Lingo can do that they won't all fit in this book. This appendix covers just a few of the Lingo terms that you can't do without: using customized cursors, checking RAM needed to play your application, how to play sounds between movies and much more.

Using Customized Cursors

Adding your own cursors can make your movie more fun, unique and easier to use. Many multimedia applications will change the cursor from an arrow to a hand when the user has placed the cursor over an item that is active. Others use a company logo or a totally individual cursor that is appropriate for the application to indicate a "hot spot." This section will show you how to use one of the 5 cursors built into Director as well as your own customized cursor.

There are 7 resources that can be used as cursors. These include a watch, , a crosshair and a crossbeam. See the Table below for the cursor number and what they are for.

0	no cursor set
-1	arrow cursor
1	I-beam cursor
2	crosshair cursor
3	crossbar cursor
4	watch cursor
200	blank cursor (no cursor)

NOTE Unfortunately, these resources cannot be used on Windows, only on a Mac. If you are creating a cross platform piece, it is recommended that you use a cast member as a cursor.

On the Mac, if you wanted to have a watch cursor display while a movie is branching from one movie to the other, use the following on stopMovie handler:

```
on stopMovie
    cursor 4
    go to movie "movie Name"
end
```

You can also change the cursor when it is over certain sprites. This is how you would indicate a hot spot by what the cursor is. In this case, the script would look like:

```
set the cursor of sprite 1 to 3.
```

You can assign any cast member as a cursor with Lingo. However, to make the most effective cursor, you need to use a 1-bit color cast member that is 16 x 16 pixels. If the cast member is larger than that, it will be cropped.

When using a cast member as a cursor you must also use a cast member as a mask. For instance, if you are using a cast member of a hand, the white pixels of the hand will be transparent. You need a mask to make the white pixel remain white. Making a mask is not hard. Just make a duplicate of the hand cast member and paint the inside of it black. The black pixels in the mask become opaque. Even if your cursor is constructed of an all-black cast member, it is still safest to mask your cursor or you may get strange results when your cursor is placed on sprites that are any color other than white.

The Lingo needed to turn a cast member into a cursor is:

```
set the cursor of sprite whichSprite to [castNumber, maskCastNumer]
```

If you want to change the cursor when it is on sprite 1 into cast member 10 using cast member 11 as the mask, the script will look like:

```
set the cursor of sprite 1 to [10,11]
```

Notice that you need to use brackets around the cast member numbers.

Playing Sounds Between Movies

A great way to enhance your application is to play some music while a new movie is loading. Impossible you say? Actually, it's quite easy using the sound playFile command. This command streams the sound file right off of a CD-ROM. This element is not even imported into your movie. To use this command, you need to specify the file, its location, and the channel you want it to play in. The interesting thing here is that you do not have only sound channel1 or sound channel2 to play it in. You can specify any sprite one of the 48 sprite channels for playback. So if you are using both sound channels in the score, you can still use this command. If you want a sound to play while another movie is loading, it is best to place this command in the on stopMovie handler. That way, no matter how the user is navigating to the second movie, the command will be executed.

Using this command will slow down the loading of the second movie. However, with the music, the user at least knows that the computer is doing something and since they have something to listen to, they often do not perceive how long the second movie takes to load.

N O T E

If you are creating a cross-platform application, make sure your sound files are saved in AIFF format so that they can play on both the Macintosh and Windows platforms.

N O T E

When you are using the sound playFile command, the sound isn't actually in the cast of your movie. This means that when you call the sound file, you need to give an exact pathName to where that sound file is located. Luckily, there is a Lingo function that makes your job easier. The function the pathName returns a string that contains the full pathName of the folder or directory in which the current movie is located. If you have a sound file called "button.aif" in a folder or sub-directory called "sounds" located within the same directory or folder as your movie, you can play it by using the following code for the Mac:

```
sound playFile 1, the pathName & "sounds:"& "button.aif"
```

For Windows, the syntax is almost exactly the same except the "\" replaces the ":" so the line of Lingo is:

```
sound playFile 1, the pathName & "sounds\"& "button.aif"
```

Remember that the ampersand (&) is a concatenator; it joins strings together.

N O T E

Memory Management Tricks

If you are creating a commercial product, you know that how much RAM the project needs is a major issue. If it requires too much RAM, you will limit the audience that can use it. How are you supposed to know how much RAM is being used? You can use the Lingo functions ramNeeded and freeBytes.

Using ramNeeded will tell you how much RAM it takes to show a certain range of frames. This function is not always as useful as you may think. Let's try a little experiment. Open the movie "MIAW1com.dir."

Open the Message Window. Type:

```
put ramNeeded (1,2)
```

Press RETURN

The above Lingo code will tell you how much RAM is needed to display the contents of frames 1 and 2.

The message window gives you a value of around 300k

Figure A.1 The RAM needed to play frames 1 and 2 of movie "MIAW1com.dir"

However, this has not taken into account how much RAM is needed to play the movies in a window. They are not in the score, so the RAM needed to play the movies in a window are not taken into effect. You can use freeBytes however to track how much memory is needed for each Movie in a Window.

FreeBytes will tell you how much RAM is available. The great thing about this function is that you can check it at various points throughout your presentation using the message window.

The value returned by freeBytes is not contiguous RAM. If you need only contiguous memory, use the Lingo function freeBlock.

N O T E

Close all windows

Open the message window.

Open the movie "MIAW1com.dir".

Play the movie.

In the message window, type "put the freeBytes" and press RETURN

Click the "Glossary" button.

In the message window, type "put the freeBytes" and press RETURN

You can see how much additional memory it takes to use a Movie in a Window.

Choose Open Notes from the Notes Menu.

Again, check the freeBytes in the message window.

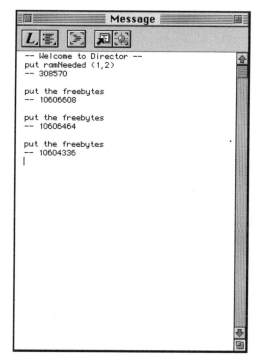

Figure A.2 The freeBytes available when playing Movies in a Window

You can see that the freeBytes is less for each window that is open. When you are investigating how much RAM is needed to play your application, take into account all the different windows that it is possible to have open at one time.

Alerting Your Audience

You saw in chapter 3 that you can play a movie in a window. One of the uses for these is for creating an alert dialog box. There is a quick and easy way to create an alert box in Lingo as well. That can be accomplished by using the alert command. The alert command will display a modal dialog box containing any message you wish along with an "OK" button. See below for an example of the alert command:

```
if the sprite = 5 then
   alert "Sorry, That Command is Not Available"
end if
```

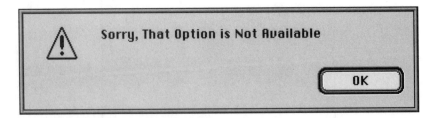

Figure A.3 An Alert Dialog Box

Unfortunately, you cannot alter the look or functionality of this Alert dialog box, so it may not always be applicable to your presentation. In that case, it's back to using Movies in a Window.

Optimizing Your Movie

When you incorporate more than one "if/then" statement, the playback head needs to check each statement to see which conditions have been met, even if the first if/then statement is true. This slows down the playback head immensely. You can speed up the performance of your application by using the case statement. The case statement is new to Director 5 and is demonstrated below.

If you had the following code:

```
if rollOver (4) then
    go to "beverage"
end if
if rollOver (5) then
    go to "Appetizer"
end if
if rollOver (6) then
    go to "entree"
end if
if rollOver (7) then
    to go "dessert"
end if
```

it could be rewritten with the case statement, making the lines of Lingo execute faster.

```
case (rollOver) of
    (4):go to "beverage"
    (5):go to "appetizer"
    (6):go to "entree"
    (7):go to "dessert"
end case
```

When using the case statement, the playback head only needs to find where the condition is true, then will not read any more lines in the case statement, but will jump down to the end case statement and start executing from there. With the if/then structure, the playback head reads through all the lines in case more than one condition is true.

Summary

Now you are a Lingo pro! You may not know every Lingo term, but you have practical experience creating a wide variety of features with Lingo for your application, from button handlers to pull down menus to navigating through cyberspace! I hope this book has been helpful to you and has given you the confidence to create exciting new multimedia presentations using Lingo. You now can explore on your own other commands and functions as you need them.

Good luck and enjoy.

INDEX

Symbols

& (concatenator), 183

¬ (continuation), 38

|, 28

— (comment), 93-94

- (separator bar), 40

A

Afterburner, 190

Alert, 214

Alphabetical Lingo tool, 75

argument,

creating 126

defining, 96, 99

B

backColor property, 67-68

Button handler, 84

Buttons, 6

    adding sound,100

    fast forward, 128, 131, 134

    glossary, 46-48

    play, 120-121

    return, 4, 16, 98

    Rewind, 128, 131-134,

X

Hey, what's on this CD-ROM?

This cross-platform CD-ROM contains completed Director 5.0 movies as well as partially assembled movies for you to work with as you use this book. Create pull down menus, view shockwave movies, learn how to implement Lingo Xtras, control QuickTime movies, create interactive presentations, use puppets for increased control, create button handlers and more!

This CD-ROM works with both Windows and Macintosh